DATE DUE

Literature and Spirit

Other Books by David Patterson

The Affirming Flame: Religion, Language, Literature, 1988
The Way of the Child (a novel), 1988
Faith and Philosophy, 1982

Translations
Winter Notes on Summer Impressions by F.M. Dostoevsky, 1988
The Forged Coupon by Leo Tolstoy, 1984
Diary of a Superfluous Man by Ivan Turgenev, 1984
Confession by Leo Tolstoy, 1983

Literature and Spirit

Essays on Bakhtin and
His Contemporaries

David Patterson

THE UNIVERSITY PRESS OF KENTUCKY

Portions of chapter 4 were published in *Cithara* 26 (May 1987), and sections of chapter 5 have appeared in the *Journal of Comparative Literature and Aesthetics* 8 (1985). The author is grateful to both periodicals for permission to reprint.

Scholarly publisher for the Commonwealth, serving Bellarmine College, Berea College, Centre College of Kentucky, Eastern Kentucky University, The Filson Club, Georgetown College, Kentucky Historical Society, Kentucky State University, Morehead State University, Murray State University, Northern Kentucky University, Transylvania University, University of Kentucky, University of Louisville, and Western Kentucky University.

Editorial and Sales Offices: Lexington, Kentucky 40506-0336

Library of Congress Cataloging-in-Publication Data

Patterson, David.
    Literature and spirit: essays on Bakhtin and his contemporaries / David Patterson.

        p. cm.
    Bibliography: p.
    Includes index.
    ISBN 0-8131-1647-3 (alk. paper)
    1. Bakhtin, M.M. (Mikhail Mikhailovich), 1895-1975.
2. Criticism—History—20th century.   I. Title.
PG2947. B3P38   1988
801′.95′0904—dc 19   88-9743

This book is printed on acid-free paper meeting the requirements of the American National Standard for Permanence of Paper for Printed Library Materials.
∞

For my wise and loving wife,
GERRI

Contents

Preface

The purpose of these essays on the Russian literary thinker Mi-khail Bakhtin (1895-1975) and a few of his contemporaries is not simply to compare but to engage his ideas in a dialogue with the ideas of others. Only in such interaction do ideas come to life. And we, the readers and respondents, must establish our presence in the midst of that interaction. This book, then, moves into a space between Bakhtin and his fellows in an effort to establish a di-alogical presence answering not only to these thinkers but to the witness who stands above all human encounter. Like any text in which truth is an issue, those texts before us put to us the question that decides the truth of ourselves: Where are you? These essays endeavor to respond, "Here I am."

A glance at the table of contents will provide an indication of the multitude of voices and viewpoints that resound in these pages. Such a variety of topics reflects both the complexity and the wealth of Bakhtin's thought. Yet the intricacies of his investigations stem from a deceptively simple concern: the spiritual dimensions of the word. It is no coincidence that such a concern leads Bakhtin to literature, for here the spiritual dimensions of the word are most pronounced. Hence the general heading under which these essays are grouped: *Literature and Spirit*, where the *and* is the word—the conjunction or the link—between literature and spirit.

The essays, however, are not merely grouped; they are inter-woven, with voices from each resonating in the others. In order to amplify that resonance, I have cited most of the figures throughout the book, and not just in the particular essays devoted to them. This method is intended to bring out the inner meanings of individual authors as well as the interrelationships among them. Certain passages from Bakhtin, it will be noted, appear in several places and in varied contexts, each one revealing a given voice or voicing in a given Bakhtinian utterance. The polyphony in this volume thus resounds between Bakhtin and his contemporaries, as well as within Bakhtin himself, despite the absence of "direct" lines of influence.

With only a few exceptions, I have confined my focus to selected primary texts. My purpose in this approach is to keep the number of voices at work in the book within manageable limits. I have also wanted to avoid making this book secondary to the secondary literature. The essays, therefore, are offered as analyses that may stand or fall according to their own merits.

Those who seek more detailed biographical information on Bakhtin will do well to consult *Mikhail Bakhtin,* by Katerina Clark and Michael Holquist, a volume that also contains a thorough and helpful bibliography.

Finally, a couple of technical points are in order. Although there seems to be little doubt that the books attributed to V.N. Voloshinov were in fact written by Bakhtin, I have nonetheless cited them according to their designated author. Unless indicated otherwise, all translations are my own. And all italics in passages quoted appear in the original text.

Introduction

Meaning is a response to a question. And the general question to which we here respond is the question of the relation between literature and spirit. In order to deal with this question, we must, of course, raise other questions. Where, for example, do we find a connection between literature and spirit? How do the two speak to and through each other? What, indeed, do we mean by *literature* and *spirit?*

Addressing this last question first, it must be noted that the term *literature* is used here in a special sense. Literature may be something written, but not just any written text qualifies as literature. Legal briefs and travel guides, for instance, are not literature. They belong to the literal, which is the opposite of the literary; they inform rather than invoke. Nor can the distinction be made along the lines separating fiction from nonfiction. Limericks and tales written solely for entertainment are not literature; their function is to divert, while the function of literature (if it can be said to be functional) is to confront and, in the light of confrontation, to affirm. Affirmation, in turn, is affirmation of truth, of what there is to hold dear, to live and die for. Literature is concerned with truth, moreover, not as something we know but as something we are or seek to become. Perhaps better: literature is characterized by a process of seeking truth and, in truth, ourselves. It is a movement toward the word within the word in an effort to get at "the man within the man."

Literature, therefore, is distinguished more by the questions that constitute its quest than by the answers that would settle its issues. Its language is the language of summons and response, a language that takes its search for truth to language itself. In a calling of deep unto deep, literature wrestles extraordinary sense from ordinary words. Through its endeavor to create through the word, it takes the word by storm to discover the mysteries of creation. If truth is the object of its quest, the word is the portal through which it passes. For the word is our only access to truth, both the truth of what we know and the truth of what we are. Literature, then, is made of word engaging word, and herein lies its dialogical dimension. A testimony that turns me into a witness, literature confronts me dialogically and insists that I respond with my own word, my own truth, my own soul. Approaching the literary text, I come up against a human voice, in responding to which I arrive at my own voice. It is a voice, in short, that puts to me the question put to the first man: Where are you?

Literature's affirmation of a truth that must be sought is thus an assignation of a responsibility that cannot be avoided. Just as truth is yet to be found, responsibility is yet to be met: literature deals with the *yet-to-be* of human life. Like the living self of the human being, its subject is always somewhere else, its kingdom always yet to come, couched in the word about to be uttered. This something other, this elsewhere, fills out the totality of meaning and is the realm of spirit. Spirit, then, has definitive connections with life and truth; to speak of one is to speak of the other. Spirit initiates and sustains the movement of literature and is revealed in the disturbance of its witness. Both textual and contextual, spirit comes into play in a space between author and character, character and reader, author and reader, always *between*, always dialogical. Forever subject, never object, spirit always interacts with itself. If literature summons response, we respond to spirit; if it announces a responsibility, we are responsible to spirit. Literature's dialogical dimensions are its spiritual dimensions. Truth is ever its topic, and spirit is its eternal witness.

In reply to—or in revision of—the question what we mean by *literature* and *spirit*, let it be said that literature and spirit are the things by which we mean and by which we have meaning, the links in life's attachment to life. Literature is composed of the word, and in the word abides the breath or the *pneuma*, the carrier and vessel of utterance. The word is the conjunction, the *and*, between literature and spirit, the scene where the two take place or are *about to* take place. The language of literature unfolds on the threshold or at the turning point of life; and in this, literature takes on the characteristics of prayer. It is an act of response that seeks a response, an expression of spiritual relation that is itself spirit. To suggest that there is a relation between literature and spirit, then, is to suggest that our relation to literature is critical indeed. In our response to literature we are confronted with a higher responsibility; deciding something about literature, we decide something about the substance and meaning of our lives. Far from being an object of academic curiosity, a question of commentary or explication, our relation to literature is a matter of spiritual life and death.

Few have been so aware of literature's profound implications for our spiritual life as Mikhail Bakhtin. Operating from a generally religious and distinctly Christian viewpoint, Bakhtin embraces the Johannine concept of the word and regards the dialogical dimensions of literature as a revelation of spirit. For Bakhtin, literature is the place where language most reveals itself and where we creatures of language most encounter ourselves. It is not surprising, therefore, that Bakhtin's religious quest into the relation between literature and spirit would lead him into the varied areas suggested by the essays in this book. He realizes, for example, that because human beings are speaking creatures, they are also laughing creatures, and that since the discourse concerning truth is always alien, it has a relation to the radically alien discourse of madness. He understands that because literature's dialogical dimensions are its spiritual dimensions, a poetics of literature is also a poetics of spirit, and that since what we are has its being through the word, the process of authoring a hero is a process of authoring a self. He sees that because the word summons a response, any self or spiritual significance we have lies in our ability to respond, that is, in our responsibility; and that since literature is continually in dialogue with life, the word is forever in dialogue with being.

One can see that the question of the relation between literature and spirit runs as deep as it does wide. Raising this question at the outset has led to still more questions, and each level of response takes us to still another issue. To be sure, this progression bespeaks the dialogical aspects of the inquiry. And because the inquiry is dialogical, it is an inquiry that takes us into ourselves. We, as much as Bakhtin and a few of his contemporaries, are the subject of this investigation. There is no human being who has not laughed, who is not implicated by madness, who is not faced with authoring a self, who does not live through the word offered to and received from others. This task, therefore, is undertaken as much in an effort to understand as in an attempt to explain. It is an endeavor to address the questions that constitute us and the responsibilities that confront us. The accent is more on the process than on the outcome. For the dialogical word is the breath by which we live; when dialogue ends, everything ends.

And so let us begin.

ONE

Bakhtin and Foucault

Laughter, Madness, Literature

Revolt is not a solution, neither is submission. Remains laughter, metaphysical laughter.

—Elie Wiesel, *Souls on Fire*

If any man come to the gates of poetry without the madness of the Muses, . . . then shall he and his works of sanity be brought to nought.

—Plato, *Phaedrus*

Mikhail Bakhtin and Michel Foucault are among those thinkers in this century who have had an impact on disciplines ranging from literary theory to cultural history. Although they did not engage in the sort of interchange that would open up issues of influence, there are certain concerns shared by the two that justify an analytical comparison of some of their ideas. Both examine elements that contribute to the evolution of literature, for example; both deal with language and discourse in relation to ideological and literary phenomena; and both investigate various forms of aberration with regard to individual and collective consciousness. In more specific terms, Bakhtin explores the role of laughter in discourse and in the novel. His book on Rabelais is particularly noteworthy in this connection, and in *The Dialogic Imagination* he identifies laughter and polyglossia, or the multitude of languages, as the two aspects of discourse that are "of decisive importance to the novel" (50-51). As we shall see below, his remarks on the menippea in *Problems of Dostoevsky's Poetics* are also of interest here. Looking at Foucault, our primary focal point will be his *Madness and Civilization*, a work in which he discusses not only the social history of madness but also its relation to discourse and creativity. Thus on the one hand we have laughter and on the other madness, with both related to discourse and verbal art. We can see, then, why Michael André Bernstein suggests this connection in his article on Bakhtin by saying, "Directly linked to this burden of terror, of laughter as a response to dread, not exuberance, is a change in the literary function of madness" (297). Hence the question arises: How are laughter, madness, and literature interrelated?

In the pages that follow, a comparison of Bakhtin and Foucault will show that laughter and madness, each involved with the other, are among the most essential contributors to the dialogical dimensions of literature; both engage the author and summon the reader to the creative act. We shall see that laughter is the peal of silence and the language of madness; that madness is the portal through which we glimpse the void underlying the creative act; and that literature is the laughing word that seeks a resolution of madness. Central to all forms of verbal art, however, are freedom of discourse and expression of truth. Freedom and truth, then, will be the touchstones that guide the ensuing discussion on the way to an understanding of laughter, madness, and literature.

LAUGHTER AND FREEDOM

The sort of laughter we are concerned with here is not the kind that comes when we feel free to laugh but the kind that sets us free. In his book on Rabelais Bakhtin calls it carnival laughter and explains, "It is, first of all, a festive laughter. Therefore it is not an individual reaction to some isolated 'comic' event. Carnival laughter is the laughter of all people. Second, it is universal in scope; it is directed at all and everyone, including the carnival's participants. The entire world is seen in its droll aspect, in its gay relativity. Third, this laughter is ambivalent: it is gay, triumphant, and at the same time mocking, deriding. It asserts and denies, it buries and revives. Such is the laughter of carnival" (11-12). This is the laughter he has in mind when he says in *Aesthetics of Verbal Art*, "Laughter lifts the barriers and opens the way to freedom" (*Estetika* 339). The primary barrier overcome by laughter is fear, the thing that holds us by the throat, and among the greatest of our fears is fear of death. Thus in *The Dialogic Imagination* Bakhtin observes, *"Death* is inseparable from *laughter"* (196). If the fear defeated by laughter is the fear of death, then laughter associated with madness and literature is born on the day we discover that we shall surely die; it is a regurgitation of the fruits of "knowledge," an undoing of the evidence of the opened eyes. While the prosaic word flees from death, the poetic word confronts death and defeats it with laughter that echoes between the lines and in the margins. Laughter opens the way to freedom not through a fugitive flight from death but through a bold and festive encounter with death. For death is always a guest at the banquet, and a skull forever lurks amid the wine cups and roses.

Thus we see that the freedom that comes with laughter is not freedom *from* but freedom *for* death. The barriers lifted are not simply those that block our way to life but those that form the fortress—or the prison—from which we would counterfeit a home; thus laughter brings us the freedom of vulnerability. While it may be true, as Martin Heidegger claims, that "freedom is freedom for grounds" (*Essence* 105), freedom for grounds is the freedom of groundlessness. This freedom clears the way for the renewed creation of artistic forms, which in turn contribute to the creation of the artist and of the self, in the open, where the future is not a source of dread but a horizon of possibility. "Freedom sets itself up against the exclusive domination of the formal element and the building of barriers," says Nicholas Berdyaev. "It presupposes the infinite" (*Dostoevsky* 73-74). In contrast to dread, the freedom for death frees the human being for the infinite *not yet* of his life, which lends meaning to his life. In this connection Bakhtin declares, "In itself, the definition given to me lies not in the categories of temporal being but in the categories of the *not-yet-existing*, in the categories of purpose and meaning, in the meaningful future, which is at odds with anything I have at hand in the past or present. To be myself for myself means becoming myself (*to cease becoming myself . . . means spiritual death*) (*Estetika* 109). I cease becoming myself whenever I live in the paralysis of fear: fear means spiritual death. We can see, then, how laughter is linked with spiritual life and how spiritual life is joined with creative life; laughter is essential to the process of becoming, and the process of becoming is essential to spiritual life. The barriers, the stone walls, removed by laughter are the walls that the rigor mortis of monological reason erects between life and itself, the "twice two is four" that Dostoevsky's underground man identified as the principle of death.

Hence the "parodic-travestying forms," to use Bakhtin's term, affected the growth of consciousness and, with it, the development of literature. As Bakhtin has noted, "These parodic-travestying forms prepared the ground for the novel in one very important, in fact decisive, respect. They liberated the object from the power of language in which it had become entangled as if in a net; they destroyed the homogenizing power of myth over language; they freed consciousness from the power of the direct word, destroyed the thick walls that had imprisoned consciousness within its own discourse, within its own language" (*Dialogic* 60). A language is a philosophy, a way of ordering the world; if what we see is owing to our metaphysics, it is owing to our language. Laughter liberates consciousness from the power of language by freeing it from the mind-molding power of metaphysics and axiological principles. Undermining the ideological outlook, laughter equally overcomes the power of myth, for there is no ideology without a mythology. While literature may take its first breath from myth, it must move beyond a given mythology if it is to sustain the process of becoming by which it lives. And as literature lives, so does consciousness, ever interacting with itself. Laughter launches us into the open and thus carries us into the depths, where we hear the alien call of deep unto deep.

The barriers penetrated by laughter, then, are those that block the way inward, and the movement inward—to what Rainer Maria Rilke calls "the depth dimension of our inner being" (see Heidegger, *Poetry* 128)—is essential to the creation and the development of literature. Indeed, the history of literature is the history of a movement inward, beyond the powers of confinement—a point that ties it to the history of madness, as Foucault suggests when he writes, "The madman is not the first and most innocent victim of confinement but the most obscure and the most visible, the most insistent of the symbols of the confining power" (*Madness* 225). Running parallel to the history of literature and the history of madness, moreover, is the history of dialogical discourse. Literature develops with the development of consciousness, and consciousness develops through dialogue with itself and with others. What occludes inwardness and would stamp us with an outward nature—the barriers themselves—is monological authority in its various forms. Such authority is the extreme expression of the fear that laughter defeats. Fear in this case is the opposite of freedom; it petrifies and paralyzes. The rigidity of authoritative, monological formulas—the fixed phrases and ready answers of authority—underscores this paralysis, while the man rollicking and dancing with laughter is the perfect image of the movement for which laughter frees us. Laughter is the sound and the fury of the soul on fire, and freedom is the flame with which it burns. The authority overcome by laughter, on the other hand, is as cold, intractable, and unresponsive as an idol of stone.

Monological authority does not seek a responsive word but rather strives to have the last word, resting on the bottom line of its self-styled syllogisms; it demands recognition, not response. Such is the word of the father as judge, carved in stone and deaf to any other word. The discourse of unreason that came to be associated with madness, however, is linked with "an attack on the Father," as Foucault puts it (*Madness* 253-54), an attack led by laughter. Along these lines Bakhtin asserts, "The authoritative word demands that we acknowledge it, that we make it our own. . . . The authoritative word is located in a distanced zone, organically connected with a past that is felt to be hierarchically higher. It is, so to speak, the word of the fathers" (*Dialogic* 342). The chain of being inevitably becomes the manacle of being, binding it to the past; the authoritative word, in fact, has only a past and not a present. The hierarchical distance is a remoteness both from the other and from the self; the dialogical word draws nigh not only the other but oneself as well. The thing that opens up the dialogical word is, again, laughter; closing the hierarchical distance, it opens up a space for the free movement toward the self by the way of the other—not the remote, authoritative other but the one who is on our own level, the one through whom one becomes I by saying "Thou." "Knowledge," in the words of Tzvetan Todorov, "takes on the form of a dialogue with a 'Thou' equal to the 'I,' yet different from the 'I' " (166). In Martin Buber's terms, laughter is the portal through which we pass from the I-It consciousness to an I-Thou consciousness.

Bakhtin has pointed out that for medieval man the victory of

laughter "was the defeat of divine and human power, of author-
itarian commandments and prohibitions, of death and punishment after death, hell and all that is more terrifying than the earth
itself. Through this victory laughter clarified man's consciousness" (*Rabelais* 90-91). Laughter's victory overcomes the ineluctable *was* of the past to free consciousness for the open-ended *not yet* of
the future, that is, to free consciousness for becoming conscious
and for the project of creating a self. Human life is no longer
defined by authority's ready answers but by the individual's constant questions; the truth is no longer something found but something sought. If consciousness is commentary, it is a commentary
that assumes the form of inquiry. In the literary realm this means
the undoing of the epic, where time is the dead time of a utopian
past in which everything has been decided and all questions
settled. Says Bakhtin, "It is precisely laughter that destroys the
epic, and in general destroys any hierarchial (distancing and
valorizing) distance" (*Dialogic* 23). He continues, "The novel took
shape precisely at the point when epic distance was disintegrating,
when both the world and man were assuming a degree of comic
familiarity, when the object of artistic representation was being
degraded to the level of a contemporary reality that was in-
conclusive and fluid" (*Dialogic* 39). Thus the change in literary
form is concurrent with a change in consciousness and in the
concepts by which we order the world before us and within us.

The waning of the epic and the waxing of the novel point up an
important relation between laughter and freedom. Here, in the
transition from medieval times to the Renaissance, laughter freed
consciousness for a new form of truth and with it a new form of
literature. Describing the Renaissance attitude toward laughter,
Bakhtin writes, "The Renaissance conception of laughter can be
roughly described as follows: Laughter has a deep philosophical
meaning, it is one of the essential forms of the truth concerning the
world as a whole, concerning history and man; it is a peculiar
point of view relative to the world; the world is seen anew, no less
(and perhaps more) profoundly than when seen from the serious
standpoint. Therefore, laughter is just as admissible in great literature, posing universal problems, as seriousness. Certain essential
aspects of the world are accessible only to laughter" (*Rabelais* 66).
The Renaissance shaking of the ground of traditions and institu-

tions could not have occurred without this view or this presence of laughter. Laughter creates difficulties and renders suspect what is settled by syllogism; bringing to bear the whole human being in reaction to reason's "twice two is four," it brings out the tension of contrasting forms that characterizes the intensity of inward life. This, indeed, is one of the fundamental aspects of the world accessible only to laughter: the inside, the underside, or the other side. If "contradiction," as Foucault argues, "functions through-out discourse, as the principle of its historicity" (*Archaeology* 151), laughter is central to the implosions of contradiction. It pursues truth in the form of disparity, in time out of joint; it seeks knowl-edge not through assimilation but through interaction.

Foucault has explained that from the Renaissance point of view knowledge consists "in bringing into being, at a level above that of all marks, the secondary discourse of commentary. The function proper to knowledge is not seeing or demonstrating; it is interpret-ing" (*Order* 40). In the Renaissance, critical activity replaced acquiescent passivity. The process of interpretation is impossible without the dialogical dimensions that laughter introduces to discourse, dimensions that we perceive in such Renaissance mas-terpieces as *Don Quixote, Gargantua and Pantagruel,* and *In Praise of Folly.* When laughter enters literature, it frees consciousness to pose questions rather than accept ready answers; assuming a sacred discontent, it exposes those who like to walk in long robes. Only in this way can the collisions that characterize the literature of Cervantes, Rabelais, Erasmus, and Shakespeare be posited. Hence we hear Bakhtin declaring that the menippea—the laugh-ing genre—"is the genre of 'ultimate questions' " (*Problems* 115). As laughter closes the gap between the self and itself, the truth it opens up becomes increasingly inward; in the words of Bakhtin, "laughter is essentially not an external but an interior form of truth" (*Rabelais* 94); rising from the belly, it takes us from the surface to the substance of human being. Because it is an interior form of truth, laughter has implications for the form that literature assumes. It frees the form to take on "a specific aesthetic relation-ship with reality," Bakhtin writes, "but not one which can be translated into logical language; that is, it is a specific means for aesthetically visualizing and comprehending reality" (*Problems* 164). In Bakhtin's view, the aesthetic relationship with reality is, moreover, a spiritual relationship, a matter concerning the soul, for "the problem of the soul," he insists, "is an aesthetic problem" (*Estetika* 89). Laughter takes us beyond logical language to religious language, here cast not in the discourse of dogma but in the outcry of the soul.

Like a sculptor who frees a living image from dead stone, laughter frees literature for the movement into those regions where we carry on the dialogue within ourselves that decides who we are and what we hold dear. This "inside," Emmanuel Levinas reminds us, "is not a secret place somewhere in me; it is that reverting in which the eminently exterior . . . concerns me and circumscribes me and orders me by my own voice" *(Otherwise* 147). Such is soliloquy. In soliloquy, Bakhtin declares, "lies the discovery of the *inner man*—'one's own self,' accessible not to passive observation but only through an *active dialogic approach to one's own self*" (*Problems* 120). The inner man or the soul of man thrives on the storm and stress of metaphysical laughter and lives as it is undermined. He who cannot laugh at himself cannot begin to know himself because he fears being undone. Taking us to the inside, laughter heals the wounds that cut the self off from itself and from others, making it hale and whole. In the movement of laughter, inside merges with outside to become one. Laughter thus joins body and soul and enables the spirit to live by the breath of the dialogical word. Only as we live in the spirit do we live in freedom and wholeness, at liberty to become more than what we are and to generate meaning in what we are *not yet*.

Contrary to what the authority of reason might tell us, the human being is whole to the extent that the *who, what,* and *where* of his life are unfinalized, to the extent that he sustains rather than settles the questions that decide his life. For the man who is free and whole, the needful task is daily confronted, yet all remains to be done. Rationalistic authority would shackle the human being with a surface nature and assess him according to what meets the eye; it is this definition and predetermination that cut the person in half, playing on the fear that eclipses the faith required to wrestle, like Jacob, with questions about ourselves and our relatons with others. Laughter casts asunder those mind-forged manacles and unlocks the way to open-ended wholeness. As Bakhtin has said, "In the whole of the world and of the people there is no room for fear. For fear can only enter a part that has been separated from the whole, the dying link torn from the link that is born. The whole of the people and of the world is triumphantly gay and fearless. This whole speaks in all carnival images" (*Rabelais* 256). Bakhtin's appeal to the people suggests why it is no coincidence that with the rise of Renaissance humanism laughter also took on a philosophical significance. His image of the link born also underscores a connection between Renaissance rebirth and the rise of metaphysical laughter. The carnival images Bakhtin refers to are the images of the laughter that engenders the freedom from fear, and this opens for us the relation to the whole whereby we become whole. The either/or at work here is either laughter or fear, either freedom or fragmentation.

Central to the carnival images are the rogue, the clown, and the fool—those who, outside the context of carnival, might be declared mad. "Essential to these figures," Bakhtin explains, "is a distinctive feature that is as well a privilege—the right to be 'other' in this world, the right not to make common cause with any single one of the existing categories that life makes available" (*Dialogic* 159). Where Bakhtin writes "right to be other" we might read *freedom* to be other, by virtue of the power of laughter to release us from the confines of existing categories. If this is a laughing matter, however, it is also a very serious matter; the more freedom, Foucault warns us, the greater the danger of madness (*Madness* 213). Berdyaev, too, realizes the danger: "There is a demonic element in man" he tells us, "for there is in him the fathomless abyss of freedom" (*Destiny* 69). Madness belongs to the demonic, the category that does not align itself with any other categories. This is a feature madness has in common with truth; like madness, truth is always an aberration, always scandalous, always other. It is from truth that laughter and madness derive their power.

MADNESS AND TRUTH

In "The Discourse on Language" Foucault writes:

From the depths of the Middle Ages a man was mad if his speech could not be said to form part of the common discourse of men. . . . And yet, in contrast to all others, his

> words were credited with strange powers of revealing some
> hidden truth; of predicting the future, of revealing, in all
> their naivete, what the wise were unable to perceive.
> . . . Whatever a madman said, it was taken for mere noise;
> he was credited with words only in a symbolic sense, in the
> theatre, in which he stepped forward, unarmed and recon-
> ciled, playing his role: that of masked truth. [*Archaeology* 217]

While Bakhtin enables us to see the significance of laughter in the
evolution of the novel, Foucault shows us the importance of madness to the literary form that undoes all form. Like the rogue, the
clown, and the fool, the madman departs from the common discourse of men by moving outside—or inside—the existing categories that life makes available. In an overflowing of meaning by
nonsense, madness penetrates the horizon of what is defined by
common discourse to open up a realm of unlimited possibility.
Here lies its power of revelation: it is the power of possibility. When
madness introduces its alien discourse, truth is cast in terms of
possibility—and therefore of freedom—rather than necessity. To
step beyond the confines of a standing discourse is precisely to step
forward unarmed, as Foucault says, for the function of the conventional is to arm and protect us from the open-ended *not yet* of
possibility. Cast in the role of veiled possibility or of masked truth,
madness is not truth so much as a sign of truth. Madness signifies
that truth is yet to be and is thus hidden, that a new vision is
required to behold it.

Sometimes the Angel of Death, the Angel with a thousand eyes,
visits a man not to take him but to leave him with a new set of eyes,
to leave him laughing, mad with his new vision of what the wise are
unable to perceive. What was once familiar grows strange; what
was once finely formed becomes deformed. Although Bakhtin
does not directly address madness to the extent that he deals with
laughter, he does have this to say: "The theme of madness is
inherent to all grotesque forms, because madness makes men look
at the world with different eyes, not dimmed by 'normal,' that is by
commonplace ideas and judgements. In folk grotesque, madness is
a gay parody of official reason, of the narrow seriousness of official
'truth.' It is a 'festive' madness" (*Rabelais* 39). When truth becomes formalized, it becomes official; when it becomes official, it

turns serious and narrow minded, empty of the passion that characterizes the quest for truth. In the rigidity and rationality of officialdom truth always degenerates into something else, into a lifeless, sleeping complacency. The monological language of commonplace ideas and judgements does not exactly hide the truth but hides the fact that something is hidden. This is the sleep that madness disturbs. "Madness begins," Foucault writes, "where the relation of man to truth is disturbed and darkened" (*Madness* 104). When the official reason Bakhtin refers to becomes the ultimate judge of truth, man's relation to truth is disturbed and darkened. Fabricating an official "truth," reason forms a mask without realizing it, its vision dimmed by the illusion of having settled matters. When we are in greatest need of him, the madman appears from the other shore to offer us a new truth, or rather a new path to truth, by donning the mask, assuming the grotesque form, that opens our eyes to the mask. The more we repress, confine, and isolate him, the more we need him. From the standpoint of officialdom, truth, again, is always in error, always mad. The truth is a fool—or a madman—riding on an ass to his certain death.

It is no coincidence that we find messianic overtones surrounding madness and its truth. The teaching through parable characteristic of the Christ is, indeed, a teaching through masks that point to the hidden. More significantly, Foucault observes that "Christ did not merely choose to be surrounded by lunatics; he himself chose to pass in their eyes for a madman, thus experiencing, in his incarnation, all the sufferings of human misfortune. Madness thus became the ultimate form, the final degree of God in man's image, before the fulfillment and deliverance of the Cross" (*Madness* 80). Although Bakhtin is operating from different perspectives, Christ has the same level of importance for him. As Clark and Holquist have noted, Christ is significant to Bakhtin "for revealing for the first time the basis of all human understanding and thus for supplying the key to understanding all things human" (86). Passing for a madman even in the eyes of the mad, Christ shows us that the path to truth does not lie in a retreat from madness but in a pursuit of madness to its very end—all the way to the Cross. The image of God in man's own image is the image of what Bakhtin terms the "inner infinity" when he says, "Life struggles to hide within itself, to go off to its inner infinity, *fears limitations,* struggles to break through them" (*Estetika* 176-77). Life struggles to penetrate one mask after another, endlessly pursuing the chain of signifiers. "Language would exceed the limits of what is thought," as Levinas expresses it, "by suggesting, letting be understood without even making understandable, an implication of meaning distinct from that which comes to signs from the simultaneity of systems or the logical definition of concepts. This possibility is laid bare in the poetic said, and in the interpretation it calls for ad infinitum" (*Otherwise* 169-70). Masked truth is truth signified; the masks of God are the images of God. And only in its final form, as the image of God in man, can madness reveal truth as that which is hidden. This is the absolute Paradox: behold the hidden!

The effort to move to the hidden side or to the inside, where the interior truth is revealed, underlies the rite of passage, so that the struggle to move inward is also a struggle to move beyond. Like Christ going into and emerging from the wilderness, the madman embarks for and returns from the other side, the place where the truth we seek is forever hidden. In his discussion of the *Narrenschiff,* or the Ship of Fools, Foucault writes:

> It is for the other world that the madman sets sail in his fool's boat; it is from the other world that he comes when he disembarks. The madman's voyage is at once a rigorous division and an absolute Passage. . . . Confined to the ship, from which there is no escape, the madman is delivered to the river with its thousand arms, the sea with its thousand roads, to that great uncertainty external to everything. He is a prisoner in the midst of what is the freest, the openest of routes: bound fast at the infinite crossroads. He is the Passenger *par excellence*: that is, the prisoner of the passage. [*Madness* 11]

The rigorous division is the division of the absolute Paradox, which posits the absolute Passage. If the absolute Passage opens the way to truth, the rigorous division forever isolates the madman from us and ourselves from truth. The task that confronts us is to make this division an occasion for dialogue; to be sure, without the division there can be no dialogue. At the infinite crossroads the great uncertainty external to everything intersects with the great uncertainty internal to everything, with the inner infinity behind the mask. This is where we collide with the absolute Other and encounter the infinite possibility within and about ourselves, for we arrive at ourselves by way of the other. Thus we set out, in Bakhtin's words, to "continually return to ourselves throughout life" (*Estetika* 17); if laughter keeps us going, madness announces the need to set out, even though we know not where to go. Art in general and literature in particular—from Homer to Joyce—are the expression of this movement of return, a movement promulgated in madness. As Plato suggests in the *Phaedrus* (492), to court the Muse is to court madness; there, where that danger lurks, poetry begins.

Set adrift in the midst of the most open of pathways, the madman reveals what is open and unsettled—two distinctive features of truth. Truth is a matter always open to dialogue, a horizon eternally unfolding. Again, the open is the interior, the realm of what Bakhtin calls *"that internally unfinalizable something in man"* (*Problems* 58). The future perfect of what we shall have been for what we are in the process of becoming takes us inward and recedes as we approach it: we stare into the abyss, and the abyss stares back. There perhaps we grow afraid; as Jacques Lacan notes, "one is never happy making way for a new truth, for it always means making our way into it: the truth is always disturbing" (*Écrits* 169). And it disturbs us at that juncture where the *not yet* of our lives proclaims itself, where, therefore, questions concerning the truth and meaning of our lives arise. This is the place or space of process and passage. To be in the process of becoming oneself is to be in a state of passage, engaged in the movement of return that characterizes the relation to the truth, which is a relation to the other. This is the revelation, the message, that the madman brings to us from the other side of the not-yet-existing: the Passenger *par excellence* is the other *par excellence*. We put out our signposts and devise our handrails to create the illusion of having settled something, to hide from the abyss of the yet-to-be, and the madman destroys them with laughter.

If he is the ultimate Passenger, moreover, the madman is also the preeminent Messenger, and his message is that there is no message, no finished and finalized truth. His message is the message Bakhtin gleans from the novels of Dostoevsky: "The catharsis that finalizes Dostoevsky's novels might be . . . expressed in this way: *nothing conclusive has yet taken place in the world, the ultimate word of the world and about the world has not yet been spoken, the world is open and free, everything is still in the future and will always be in the future*" (*Problems* 166). The madman's message, finally, is that the message lies in the questions we raise and not in the conclusions we settle upon. What Foucault refers to as the freest and most open of routes we recognize in Bakhtin as the road that goes into the world, open and free. To be sure, "the importance of the chronotope of the road in literature," as he declares in *The Dialogic Imagination,* "is immense" (98). For the road is full of the bends and crossroads that launch everything into the future. The past is marked with the footprints or the imprints of the already said, while the future belongs to the process of saying and becoming. "Language always seems to be inhabited by the other, the elsewhere, the distant," Foucault points out. "It is hollowed by absence" (*Archaeology* 111). Language is inhabited by the unuttered future word, and the utterance of the madman is the utterance of the elsewhere and the distant that collapses the distance of hierarchical authority. The ambivalent laughter of the madman thus purifies us of the authoritative past, of the epic past. Like the mad Baptist, he comes to wash away the old forms, to prepare new bottles for a new wine. Here we are reminded of what Foucault has observed: "Water and madness have long been linked in the dreams of European man" (*Madness* 12). Water is the face of the deep that summons the deep within, the medium of passage and purification.

And so the sequence that underscores the relation between madness and truth unfolds: passage, message, baptism. In the rite of purification, which is a rite of passage, we become other through the mediation of the other. If, as Bakhtin has said, "two voices is the minimum for life, the minimum for existence" (*Problems* 252), it is because the I requires the other in order to become what he is not yet. One does not imply two, but rather two are required to form one, with truth present as an invisible third, as we shall see below. To the extent that truth is not what we try to find out but what we endeavor to become, it is relegated to the realm of the not-yet-existing; truth is something other, something elsewhere, and any relation of an I to truth turns on a relation of the I to the other. Encountering the other, I encounter myself as other and perceive myself through other eyes and ears, thus stepping outside myself, moving elsewhere, to gauge my relation to truth. This is precisely what the author of a literary work must do, if his work is to voice a truth or lay bare a lie; as Bakhtin has noted, the author "must become *other* to himself, must look upon himself through the eyes of another" (*Estetika* 16). Literature is the work of an author, and the work of an author is passage, message, and baptism: he passes through himself by way of his character in an effort to bear witness, to respond as he has been summoned, making his response into a summons. And in his act of creation he is himself created. The task confronting the author, then, confronts every self, every soul: self-creation.

The project of becoming other to oneself is a project of shifting from one's own discourse to the discourse of the other. This movement, we read in *The Dialogic Imagination,* opens up "the possibility of translating one's own intentions from one linguistic system into another, of fusing 'the language of truth' with 'the language of the everyday,' of saying 'I am me' in someone else's language, and in my own language, 'I am other' " (315). To say "I am me" in someone else's language is precisely to say, "I am other" in my own language; as soon as my language becomes other, so do I. Only by thus placing myself in the position of the other can I return to the truth of myself. Truth is recognized by its power to disturb the one who is its witness, throwing him back on himself and making him noncoincident with himself. And truth draws its power from discourse, where "discourse is not the majestically unfolding manifestation of a thinking, speaking subject," as Foucault has said, "but, on the contrary, a totality, in which the dispersion of the subject and his discontinuity with himself may be determined" (*Archaeology* 55). The encounter with the other is an encounter with the discourse of the other. Like the life of the word, the life of the living individual proceeds along a path of shifting contexts, of shifting voices, in the dialogical interaction with the other. Hence we discover that, as the most extreme case of the other and of the alien discourse, the madman is the most essential to the I's relation to truth and therefore to literature's ability to address truth, which, indeed, is what literature is about. As Bakhtin points out, the clown and the fool come to the aid of the novelist in meeting the task of exposing "all that is vulgar and falsely stereotyped in human relationships" (*Dialogic* 162). Indeed, Bakhtin insists, the novelist's primary task is to become other to himself (*Estetika* 16). Because the discourse of the clown and the fool—the discourse of the madman—is most alien, it most questions and sustains the novelist's process of becoming other to himself, the process that forms the basis of his relation to truth.

In *The Dialogic Imagination* Bakhtin writes, "The word is born in a dialogue as a living rejoinder within it; the word is shaped in dialogic interaction with an alien word" (279). The nuances of an utterance belong both to the speaker and to the listener, as well as to their linguistic milieu. An important ramification of Bakhtin's statement can be found in *The Archaeology of Knowledge,* where Foucault says that the word or discourse cannot be defined "by recourse to a transcendental subject nor by recourse to a psychological subjectivity" (55). The significance of madness, then, lies in its impact on discourse as both the realm and the hiding place of truth. "*Representation* in the image," says Foucault, "is not enough; it is also necessary to *continue* the delirious *discourse*. For in the patient's insane words there is a voice that speaks; it obeys its own grammar, it articulates a meaning" (*Madness* 188). Having said this much, we can pursue the matter a bit further and say that the dialogical word essential to truth is born in the interaction with the alien word of madness. The interaction between word and alien word is the paradigm for truth conceived not as what is found but as what is sought. The former belongs to authoritative monologue, the latter to existential dialogue. "The dialogic means of seeking the truth," Bakhtin tells us, "is counterposed to *official* monologism, which pretends to *possess a ready-made truth*" (*Problems* 110). If truth is born in the interaction between word and alien word, then the official as "the one who knows"—indeed, any knowing subject—is deposed. In the light of this threat, the ready-made "truth" of officialdom seeks to stifle the alien discourse by deeming it mad; one need only recall those countries today where opposition to the party line is enough to have a person declared insane. Yet truth lives in this opposition of discourses.

As something sought in dialogue, truth is the opposite of the ready-made; as something opposed to the ready-made, truth is not what we know but what we are *not yet*. "A man never coincides with himself," Bakhtin explains. "One cannot apply to him the formula A = A. In Dostoevsky's artistic thinking, the genuine life of the personality takes place at the point of non-coincidence between a man and himself. . . . "The genuine life of the personality is made available only through a *dialogic* penetration of that personality" (*Problems* 59). Insofar as we live, we are in process, our lives characterized by the movement of quest and question, by the rite of passage through ourselves. Ever changing, never self-coinciding, we move from one encounter to another, repeatedly confronting the task of overcoming the monological outlook. At that point of confrontation madness is both the great danger and the grand inquisitor. In its counterposition to official monologism, madness brings us to the crossroads of noncoincidence with ourselves. Here we undertake the dialogue with madness, with the utterly alien word, that launches us into the inner regions of ourselves, not as psychological subjects but as beings who live in the dialogical word, the dwelling place of the genuine life of truth. Thus we discover again that the alien discourse of madness, the word from the other shore, leads us to the inside or the other side of life; it takes us toward the realm of truth, not by way of agreement but by way of contradiction. In the words of Foucault, "discourse is the path from one contradiction to another" (*Archaeology* 151). Dialogue is a means of seeking truth that is never equal to itself, and it cannot do without madness.

When madness is drawn into a relation with truth, truth becomes a live event, noncoincident with itself, and not a dead datum. If we may associate truth with idea, moreover, then what Bakhtin says of the idea may also be said of truth: "The idea *lives* not in one person's *isolated* individual consciousness—if it remains there only, it degenerates and dies. The idea begins to live . . . only when it enters into genuine dialogic relationships with other ideas, with the ideas of *others*" (*Problems* 87-88). The other idea, which brings the truth out of isolation and thus breathes life into it, is madness. The most extreme and therefore the most genuine dialogue is the dialogue with madness, for madness is what makes word and idea a living dialogical event. The "two or several consciousnesses" Bakhtin refers to in the following are, in the most radical instance, the consciousness of man and madman: "The idea is a *live event,* played out at the point of dialogic meeting between two or several consciousnesses. In this sense the idea is similar to the *word,* with which it is dialogically united. Like the word, the idea wants to be heard, understood, and 'answered' by other voices from other positions. Like the word, the idea is by nature dialogic" (*Problems* 88). United with the word dialogically, the idea is as much a question as it is an answer; it both responds and seeks a response—not only from the other but from "the eternal silence of these infinite spaces" that so terrified Pascal (95). If the madman begins with raving, he often ends with silence. And if in the dialogue with madness the void thus makes itself heard, it is the void within ourselves that we hear. We come to consciousness in this meeting with the alien consciousness of madness, and through that encounter we become conscious of the silent void. This is where the need for the word, for critical response, announces itself; this is where the longing of the demiurge to creativity is revealed. And because that longing is revealed through dialogue, creativity here takes the form of discourse, of literature.

LITERATURE AND CREATION

At this point we may address the question how laughter and madness combine to influence the development of the discourse that constitutes literature. Laughter frees consciousness from the confines of its own discourse, and this freedom is the first prerequisite for the creation of literature. In order to create anything one must first be free to be other and to become something other. It is only from a position of otherness that literature can generate its dialogue with life. In the words of Bakhtin, the freedom born of laughter is what enables literary discourse to engage in "an uninterrupted mutual interaction with the discourse of life" (*Dialogic* 303). Why? Because, as Bakhtin notes, "it is in the word that laughter manifests itself most variously" (*Dialogic* 236-37). Here we may call to mind parodies and puns, satires and asides, all of which are examples of literary forms of discourse riddled with laughter in interaction with life. Laughter thus manifested in the word is not simply a reaction but is a response that in turn seeks a response. Laughter, then, is a form of discourse that turns discourse back on itself. If laughter manifests itself most variously in the word, it also introduces variation and deviation to the word itself.

Coupling Bakhtin's insight with the following observation made by Foucault in *Madness and Civilization,* we see that the bond that links laughter and madness ultimately influences the creation of literature as discourse:

> Madness, in the classical sense, does not designate so much a specific change in the mind or in the body, as the existence, under the body's alterations, under the oddity of conduct and conversation, of *a delirious discourse.* . . . Language is the first and last structure of madness, its constituent form; on language are based all the cycles in which madness articulates its nature. That the essence of madness can be ultimately defined in the simple structure of a discourse does not reduce it to a purely psychological nature, but gives it a hold over the totality of soul and body. [99-100]

Madness is not simply a state of mind signified by discourse but is the chain of signifiers that constitutes a discourse out of joint. In the midst of "the freest, the openest of routes" madness freely takes the signifiers of discourse along new and deviant paths, making no "common cause with any single one of the existing categories." These new paths and uncommon categories are those of creativity. The delirious discourse of madness is a laughing discourse, and the literary word is the laughing word. For if discourse gives madness a hold over the totality of body and soul, so does it give literature such a hold, inasmuch as literature is in constant interaction with the discourse of life; and festive, affirming laughter—the laughter that defeats death—is at the center of that interaction. Because laughter and madness are manifested in language, they enable literature to put its questions to life; they lend literature the otherness that is the essence and issue of creation and that brings us to the edge of nothingness.

The literary word that opens up the abyss lying at our feet, then, derives its power from madness. In this connection Foucault de-

clares, "By the madness which interrupts it, a work of art opens a
void, a moment of silence, a question without answer, provokes a
breach without reconciliation where the world is forced to question itself" (*Madness* 288). The silent word, the breach without
reconciliation, both summons and responds in the literary word. It
hears as it speaks, laughs as it hears. The distinguishing chronotope in literature—that critical juncture of space and time
where encounter occurs—is thus the threshold, and, Bakhtin explains, "its most fundamental instance is as the chronotope of *crisis*
and *break* in a life" (*Dialogic* 248). If madness provokes such a
breach, it does so with the help of the laughter that undoes our
"truths" and thus poses a question without answer; if the work of
art opens a moment of silence, laughter is the peal of that silence.
Abruptly bursting forth, laughter announces the breach without
reconciliation and introduces a fearsome *suddenness* to life. Questioning the fixed truths about our nature, laughter joins with
madness to reveal what Foucault calls "the infinity of non-nature"
(*Madness* 284), the open horizon of all that is other to the artificial
arrangement of reality we term nature. Hence we collide with
nothingness, a nothingness that is not a mute emptiness but
something that serves as the backdrop for creation and with which
literary discourse continually interacts. Says Foucault, "Joining
vision and blindness, image and judgement, hallucination and
language, sleep and waking, day and night, madness is ultimately
nothing, for it unites in them all that is negative. But the paradox of
this *nothing* is to *manifest* itself, to explode in signs, in words, in
gestures" (*Madness* 107). The variant paths in the established
chain of signifiers converge to form the deviant paths of madness:
the explosion is a fusion reaction that marks a beginning—a
threshold. And a beginning, in the words of Heidegger, "always
contains the undisclosed abundance of the unfamiliar and extraordinary, which means that it also contains strife with the
familiar and ordinary" (*Poetry* 76). With literature, indeed, everything begins and nothing ends.

Creation is precisely the linkage of the disparate, and in literature it achieves its highest form or manifestation in the novel. "In
the process of becoming the dominant genre," Bakhtin argues,
"the novel sparks the renovation of all other genres, it infects them
with its spirit of process and inconclusiveness" (*Dialogic* 7). We

recall in this connection the importance Bakhtin attaches to the interaction of a familiar discourse with an alien discourse in the development of the novel. Foucault renders this encounter of the alien with the familiar in terms of perversion. "The novel," he writes in *Madness and Civilization,* "constitutes the milieu of perversion, *par excellence,* of all sensibility; it detaches the soul from all that is immediate and natural in feeling and leads it into an imaginary world of sentiments violent in proportion to their unreality" (219). The violence Foucault speaks of is violence done in the undoing of the authoritative reality; creation is in this sense an act of violence, a certain crime, a stealing of fire from the gods. The "infinity of non-nature" invades the finitude of "nature" to overturn all that is "natural in feeling" and to turn the soul over to "unreality" or to all that is alien to a conventional reality. Hence the novel does not engage in monological description or prescription but in dialogical encounter and collision. While Bakhtin reveals the role of laughter in that encounter, Foucault unearths the function of madness in that collision. From the clown to the lunatic, laughter and madness commence in perversion and end in creation.

Bakhtin has observed that "to a greater or lesser extent, every novel is a dialogical system made up of the images of 'languages,' styles and consciousnesses that are concrete and inseparable from language. Language in the novel not only represents, but itself serves as the object of representation. Novelistic discourse is always criticizing itself" (*Dialogic* 49). If the literary word is the laughing word, in the novel it laughs at itself. In the evolution of literature, the undoing of form through a self-critique of form corresponds to what Foucault terms "the disparity between the awareness of unreason and the awareness of madness." Here unreason is akin to a force that continually returns to threaten reason, while madness is situated in a temporal sequence of development. Just as laughter becomes a motif, madness becomes a method. Says Foucault.

In the disparity between the awareness of unreason and the awareness of madness, we have, at the end of the eighteenth century, the point of departure for a decisive movement: that by which the experience of unreason will continue, with Hölderlin, Nerval, and Nietzsche, to proceed ever deeper

toward the roots of time—unreason thus becoming, *par excellence,* the world's *contratempo*—and the knowledge of madness
seeking on the contrary to situate it ever more precisely
within the development of nature and history. It is after this
period that the time of unreason and the time of madness
receive two opposing vectors: one being unconditional return
and absolute submersion; the other, on the contrary, developing according to the chronicle of a history. [*Madness*
212]

The two opposing vectors Foucault refers to appear in the tension
between creation and literature. On one hand, the act of creation
contains an element of return to the Creation, and, as we have
noted, literature abounds in the theme of return. On the other
hand, we find in literature's creation and eclipse of form a development according to a chronicle of history. Whether we place the
accent on return or on development, we have a sense of path or
road; it is no coincidence that, again, we find Bakhtin emphasizing
the importance of the chronotope of the road in literature (*Dialogic*
98). In taking up a direction, madness becomes chronotopic as it
becomes a counterpoint to the time and place of the world. We
recall once more the rite of passage that Foucault associates with
madness (*Madness* 11). Literature is the Ship of Fools moving
forward and sounding as it goes the depths of the origin of all
things created by the word.

In *The Order of Things* Foucault asserts that "the original in man
is that which articulates him from the very outset upon something
other than himself. . . . What is conveyed in the immediacy of the
original is, therefore, that man is cut off from the origin that would
make him contemporaneous with his own existence" (331-32). He
goes on to remind us that "what we are concerned with here is
neither a completion nor a curve, but rather that ceaseless rending
open which frees the origin in exactly that degree to which it
recedes; the extreme therefore is what is nearest" (334). Whether it
is the path of return or the course of development, the road posits
the beginning; the origin is reestablished at every crossroads,
every threshold, every site of the rending open. These breaks in life
bring to mind the moments of crisis that, Bakhtin observes, distinguish the characters in Dostoevsky's novels (*Problems* 61); these are

people for whom the extreme is indeed the nearest. One example Foucault cites to connect the chronicle of madness with that of literature is the case of the Marquis de Sade: "Sadism appears at the very moment that unreason, confined for over a century and reduced to silence, reappears, no longer as an image of the world, no longer as *figura*, but as language and desire. And it is no accident that sadism, as an individual phenomenon bearing the name of a man, was born of confinement and, within confinement, that Sade's entire *oeuvre* is dominated by images of the Fortress, the Cell, the Cellar, the Convent" (*Madness* 210). These images of confinement are counterposed to the open road, to the rending open, of madness. Here the movement forward is expressed as a movement inward, toward the center or the seed of language and desire. Madness and unreason take up two opposing vectors to merge in literature, where we find an effort to return by moving forward in a historical development. As the voice of absolute otherness, madness announces the need to become other; as the creative word, literature is the expression of that process of becoming, and it takes its impetus from laughter. If the gods laughed themselves to death, it is for man to laugh himself to life.

The project of literature and creation, then, is rebirth; this event is the aim of return through movement forward, the point of intersection for the two opposing vectors of madness and unreason. It is signaled by the regenerative power of laughter, as in the case of the birth of Isaac, whose name means "he has laughed." Recall in this connection Bakhtin's insight on carnival's hell as a kind of cosmic womb: "Carnival's hell represents the earth which swallows up and gives birth, it is often transformed into a cornucopia; the monster, death, becomes pregnant. Various deformities, such as protruding bellies, enormous noses, or humps, are symptoms of pregnancy or of procreative power. Victory over fear is not its abstract elimination; it is a simultaneous uncrowning and renewal, a gay transformation. Hell has burst and has poured forth abundance" (*Rabelais* 91). As the world's contratempo, however, the spectre of madness places rebirth forever in the realm of the yet-to-be, beyond all existing categories and horizons. Thus we may glimpse the significance of Foucault's cryptic remark that "madness is childhood" (*Madness* 252). Childhood is both seed and generation, both point of origin and vessel of development. It is

pure potentiality, the realm of open-ended possibility, which madness proclaims and which creation seeks; recall, for example,
Nietzsche's three stages of metamorphosis outlined in *Thus Spoke
Zarathustra*—camel, lion, and child—which he associates with submission, revolt, and creation (559). Sade's cell and convent are
images of confinement, but they are also images of the womb.
When madness takes up the vector of historical development, it
situates itself, like childhood, in temporality, which, Bakhtin argues, "confronts meaning as *yet-to-be-fulfilled*, as *not-all-over-yet*"
(*Estetika* 107).

We have seen that madness unsettles and laughter sets into
motion; both point up a process of becoming, in which meaninglessness is not just a condition of the world but the condition
from which the world must be delivered. Meaning is a state of
becoming, and this is what underlies creation in general and
literature in particular. For "creation always goes with a change in
meaning," Bakhtin has observed (*Estetika* 342), and a change in
meaning always goes with a change in consciousness and in life.
Thus, Bakhtin realizes, "I live in the depths of myself through faith
and hope in the ongoing possibility of the inner miracle of a new
birth" (*Estetika* 112). To live in the depths of myself is to live in a
process of becoming; laughter opens up those depths, and madness sounds them out. And performing the miracle of rebirth is the
work of creation and literature.

The project of rebirth requires what Bakhtin regards as a
"special responsibility" in creation and expression. In his essay
"Author and Hero in Aesthetic Activity," for example, he writes,
"Wherever the alibi becomes a prerequisite for creation and expression, there can be no responsibility, no seriousness, no meaning. A special responsibility is required . . . ; but this responsibility
can be founded only on a profound belief in a higher truth, . . . the
belief that another, higher being responds to my special responsibility, that I do not act in an utter void. Apart from this belief
there can be only empty pretense" (*Estetika* 179). The laughter that
questions monologism and the madness that poses the absolute
Passage imply the higher truth to which literature is answerable.
Undertaking the creation of meaning, the author must meet a
responsibility to the Creator, who is the source of meaning. New
meaning and new life cannot happen without the relation to the

higher truth. Literature, then, is not so much a new arrangement of signs as it is itself a sign of that to which it answers. How do I know I do not act in an utter void? Why do I have faith in the inner miracle of a new birth? Because I create. Because I not only give signs but become a sign: my response is also a summons. This is what is special, what is dialogical, about the special responsibility. Because it is dialogical, the special responsibility is forever to be met, and no one can answer for me.

If the author stands in a responsive relation to a higher being, then so does the reader; rebirth is a task that not only confronts the author but faces the reader as well. Like the author, the reader is called to participate in the creation of the literary work, so that, in Bakhtin's words, "the event in the life of the text—that is, its genuine essence—develops *along the boundary between two consciousnesses*" (*Estetika* 285). Like the author, the reader must become other, noncoincident with himself, by opening up the discourse of himself to the discourse of the other. In one of his notes from 1970-71, Bakhtin brings out an important implication of this: "Understanding fills out the text: it is active and takes on a creative character. Creative understanding continues creativity" (*Estetika* 346). The reader's active, creative relation to the text is part of his own self-creation, which is a process of listening and responding. Coming before a literary text, the reader comes to a threshold or turning point in his process of becoming, so that through his relation to the text he decides something about the meaning of his life. And because each individual self lives and dies in relation to a world, the responsive relation to the text affects the arrangement of life and death in the world. Hence in *The Dialogic Imagination* we hear Bakhtin declare, "The work and the world represented in it enter the real world and enrich it, and the real world enters the work and its world as part of the process of its creation, as well as part of its subsequent life, in a continual renewing of the work through the creative perception of listeners and readers" (254). Literature is not mimetic; it does not mirror the world but interacts with it in a manner that transforms both the work and the world, both author and reader, who are responsible for that transformation. Again, laughter and madness posit this responsibility.

At this point we should recall the connection that Foucault

draws between madness in literature and the responsibility that literature poses for the world: "There is no madness except as the final instant of the work of art—the work endlessly drives madness to its limits; *where there is a work of art, there is no madness;* and yet madness is contemporary with the work of art, since it inaugurates the time of its truth. The moment when, together, the work of art and madness are born and fulfilled is the beginning of the time when the world finds itself arraigned by that work of art and responsible before it for what it is" (*Madness* 288-89). The delirious discourse of madness becomes the literary discourse of the text as the author drives his own language to the limits of language, where the silence of the unuttered truth is heard. As a response to madness, the literary work is a resolution of madness; and because madness is the thing resolved, it defines the work's relation to truth. This relation poses the question of our relation to truth, so that madness and literature join to summon the response and responsibility of the reader and his world. If discourse here "gives rise to those [contradictions] that can be seen," to borrow again from Foucault, "it is because it obeys that which it hides" (*Archaeology* 151). Like the relation between the discourse of madness and the discourse of literature, then, the relation between text and reader is dialogical. And since the relation between the two is dialogical, both stand in a relation to a third position, which is the silent place of the hidden, unuttered truth. Listen to Bakhtin: "Every dialogue proceeds as though against the background of a responsive understanding of a third who is invisibly present, standing above all the participants in the dialogue. . . . The third referred to here has nothing to do with mysticism or metaphysics . . . it is a constitutive feature of the whole expression" (*Estetika* 306). The third here represents the position of truth which is yet to be uttered. It is by virtue of the third that madness inaugurates the time of truth in the literary work; without the third, madness has no connection with the work, and the reader has nothing to answer for. And laughter? The literary work is its echo, for there is no literature, no creation, except as the final instant of laughter.

Thus we arrive at the interconnection posed at the outset: laughter, madness, literature. With the combined help of Bakhtin and Foucault, we penetrate a surface beyond which neither thinker leads us by himself. Seeing the one bring out a link between laughter and literature and the other the mediation between madness and literature, we find that the literary word is not only the laughing word but the mad word, the organized outcry, of the I who comes before the countenance of the third, of "the over-*I*— that is, the witness and judge of every man (of every *I*)" to use Bakhtin's phrase (*Estetika* 342). We also find that if madness and laughter are indispensable constituents of the author's activity, they are also essential to the reader's response. One is reminded of Bakhtin's remark that "I must answer for what I have experienced and understood in art with my very life. . . . Art and life are not one and the same, but they must become one within me, in the wholeness of my responsibility" (*Estetika* 5-6). And they cannot become one within me unless I become other than what I am in a movement to where I am not yet, to the other shore: in order to become whole, I must become a bridge. In the wholeness of my responsibility, I draw the literature into my life by appropriating enough of the delirious discourse to transform my own discourse and enough of the laughter to call that discourse—and myself— into question.

If we do not quake at the way here set forth, then we do not understand it. As Foucault has pointed out, madness has become "the end and the beginning of everything. Not because it is a promise, as in German lyricism, but because it is the ambiguity of chaos and apocalypse" (*Madness* 281). The great danger, Foucault goes on to say, is that "madness is the absolute break with the work of art; it forms the constitutive moment of abolition, which dissolves in time the truth of the work of art; it draws the exterior edge, the line of dissolution, the contour against the void" (287). It is from this edge of the forest of the night that we must reach into the void to fetch the trace of the fugitive truth. There we collide with nothingness and meet the task of responding with a dialogical word, of burning with an affirming flame; there we encounter the ambiguous and dangerous Perhaps invoked by Kierkegaard and Nietzsche. The truth of the art turns on this critical interaction with it, and the truth of who and where I am turns on the truth of the art. Both the author's and the reader's relation to the literary word—conceived in laughter and mediated by madness—entails a higher relation and a deeper responsibility to the word: the act of response becomes an act of courage and a matter of spiritual life and death.

The ties that bind laughter, madness, and literature, therefore, are spiritual and suggest a poetics of spirit that must be worked out in fear and trembling. For it is a poetics of unsettled truth, and in deciding something about such a poetics we decide something about ourselves as well. Like body and soul, form and idea here combine to beckon and constitute the spiritual dimension of literature and of life. The event that takes place in literature, as Bakhtin states it, in *Aesthetics and Theory of the Novel* is "a spiritual activity of the production and selection of sense, of connections, of axiological relations; it is the inner tension of a spiritual contemplation" (*Esthétique* 79-80). This position, indeed, provides the basis for Bakhtin's treatment of Dostoevsky's poetics and for the approach to Dostoevsky's ideas taken by Berdyaev and Gide.

TWO

Bakhtin, Berdyaév, and Gide

Dostoevsky's Poetics of Spirit

In *Problems of Dostoevsky's Poetics*, Bakhtin argues that in Dostoevsky's novels an idea is "neither a *principle of representation* (as in any ordinary novel), nor the leitmotif of representation, nor a conclusion drawn from it (as in a novel of ideas or a philosophical novel); it is, rather, the *object of representation*" (24). The title of his book on Dostoevsky might suggest that Bakhtin is concerned more with the author's poetics than with his message, more with the *how* than with the *what* of the idea. Yet his approach to Dostoevsky is based on a connection between the manner in which the idea unfolds and the content of the idea; to be sure, it is an approach that renders suspect the separation of form and idea. In his essay "The Problem of Verbal Genres" Bakhtin is quite explicit on this point: "Style," he argues, "is directly connected with determined thematic unities and—what is especially important—with determined compositional unities" (*Estetika* 242). And he states his thesis in "Discourse in the Novel" by saying, "The principle idea of this essay is that the study of verbal art can and must overcome the divorce between an abstract 'formal' approach and an equally abstract 'ideological' approach" (*Dialogic* 259). Bringing out the dialogical dimensions of Dostoevsky's novels, Bakhtin's investigation is itself dialogical and conveys a "potential other meaning, that is, the loophole left open," which "accompanies the word like a shadow" (*Problems* 233). Alongside his theory of the novel he develops a discourse on truth; with his examination of character he presents a concept of self. Thus we find a polyphony of ideas at work in Bakhtin's treatment of Dostoevsky's poetics, so that his work is both testimonial and analytical.

The message to which Bakhtin bears witness is to a large extent the one that Nicholas Berdyaev and André Gide convey in their own investigations. One could, for instance, describe Bakhtin's book on Dostoevsky in words similar to those Gide uses to portray his study of the Russian author: "It will be, just as much as a book of criticism, a book of confessions, to anyone who knows how to read; or rather, a profession of faith" (xi). Although Bakhtin operates from a very different perspective and would surely have much to add, he would probably agree with Gide's claim that "ideas are all that is most precious in Dostoevsky" (xii). Berdyaev, too, places his accent on ideas in Dostoevsky. He may not use the same terms that Gide does, but his purpose is the same, namely, "to display Dostoevsky's spiritual side" (*Dostoevsky* 11). This, indeed, is precisely what Bakhtin achieves, perhaps even more so than Berdyaev or Gide, for Bakhtin explores discourse or the word with the view that the word is spirit.

Again similar to Berdyaev and Gide, Bakhtin proceeds from a Christian standpoint; it will be recalled, for instance, that he was exiled to Kustani in 1930 for his involvement in a Christian group known as Voskresenie. While Berdyaev and Gide openly assume a Christian position, Bakhtin found it necessary to do so by implication in his early works, although his Christian bent does come out quite clearly in *Aesthetics of Verbal Art* (see *Estetika* 51-52). More specifically, Berdyaev and Bakhtin embrace a Johannine Christianity, with Berdyaev invoking the Johannine Spirit (see *Dostoevsky* 207) and Bakhtin citing the Johannine Word (see *Estetika* 357). In her preface to Bakhtin's *Problems of Dostoevsky's Poetics*, Caryl Emerson points out that Bakhtin's endeavor, in fact, is "a basically religious quest into the nature of the Word" (xxxi). And in *Mikhail Bakhtin*, Clark and Holquist write, "This conviction that the sign has a body corresponds to Bakhtin's ontotheological view that the spirit has a Christ. The kenotic event that is reenacted in language is the mode of God's presence to human beings" (225). The kenotic event—the spirit or word made flesh—is the key to the approaches to Dostoevsky taken by Bakhtin, Berdyaev, and Gide. All three, each in his own way, are concerned with the spiritual dimensions of Dostoevsky and with literature as spirit.

The ensuing comparison of Bakhtin, Berdyaev, and Gide in their investigations of Dostoevsky will show that the dialogical dimensions of Dostoevsky's art are its spiritual dimensions, with both aspects intersecting in the word. The discourse and form of his novels are essential to the ideas they address, a point that Gide no doubt wants to make when he declares, "Had he been philosopher instead of novelist, he would certainly have attempted to bring his ideas into line, whereby we should have lost the most precious of them" (51). The ideas in this case cannot be brought into line, if that means conformed to the reason that rules speculative philosophy. They require, instead, the delirious discourse of the novel, just as the spirit needs storm and dizziness. In Dostoevsky's novels concept is involved with structure, message with poetics, literature with spirit. Setting up a dialogue among the three thinkers before us, we shall see that spiritual truth takes on polyphonic form and that the literary effort to penetrate the personality is also a religious endeavor. Before us, then, is "a meditation on the mysteries inherent in God's making people and people's making selves, with the activity of people creating other people in literary authorship as a paradigm for thinking at all levels of creating" (Clark and Holquist 80). Before us, in short, is a poetics of spirit. And the stake is spiritual life.

POLYPHONIC FORM

In their discussion of the Kantian features of Bakhtin's thought, Clark and Holquist tell us, "The systematic aspects of language are to speech as the material world is to mind. Thus they differ from each other but always operate together. The two sets of features interact in a dynamic unity and cannot without conceptual violence be separated from each other. The arena where they intermingle and the force that binds them are both what Bakhtin understands by 'utterance' " (222). Similarly, we are here viewing the novel as an arena, as well as a force, of interaction. It is a framework of discourse in which a multitude of voices are brought together for dialogical intermingling. The manner in which those voices are set off one against the other—the *here* and *there* of their arrangement—constitutes the novel's polyphonic form. When dealing with polyphonic form, then, we deal with a spatial rather than a chronological structure, a point that Bakhtin stresses with respect to Dostoevsky's novels (*Problems* 28).

The spatial structure is not simply an aesthetic device but is a definitive feature of the novel's discourse itself. "Words have their *locus*," Foucault maintains, "not in *time*, but in a *space* in which they are able to find their original site, change their positions, turn back upon themselves, and slowly unfold a whole developing curve: a *tropological* space" (*Order* 114). Organized according to an interchange of words, Dostoevsky's novels are built around characters that determine *who* they are according to *where* they are situated in relation to another character. The problem of presence, the problem of making life one with the word, is the problem of being able to respond, "Here I am," when standing before the other. Recall, for example, the imperative Kirillov, in *The Possessed*, puts to Verkhovensky when he says, "If the laws of nature did not spare even *Him*, did not spare even their miracle, but made Him live in a lie and die in a lie, then the whole planet is a lie and rests on a lie and a stupid mockery. Thus the very laws of this world are a lie and a vaudeville of devils. What is there to live for? Answer if you're a man!" (*Besy* 642-43). And then there are questions such as the one Ivan puts to Alyosha in *The Brothers Karamazov:* "I want to be there when everyone finds out what all this has been for. All the religions of the earth are founded on this longing, and I am a believer. But then there are the children, you see, and what am I supposed to do about them?" (*Brat'ya* 267). In Dostoevsky's novels, being there always means being *with*, or better: being *for*. Confronted with the task of living in his word, each character meets the difficulty of being present before another; each must transfer his life blood into his voice through a response, in word or deed, to another voice.

We must bear this in mind when we hear Bakhtin say, "The fundamental category in Dostoevsky's mode of visualizing was not evolution, but *coexistence* and *interaction*. He saw and conceived his world primarily in terms of space, not time" (*Problems* 28). Again, as crossroads and turning points become more important in literature, the stasis of epic time gives way to the dynamic of novelistic space; the novel makes room for the alien word, or the voice of the other, and creates a space where dialogue can occur. The dialogue is not in time but rather time is in the dialogue. When voice coexists with voice and word interacts with word, the chronological collapses into the instant, not as a particle of time but as an atom of eternity. Everything hangs on the word of the other and on my response to that word; hence Golyadkin's torment over Krest'yan Ivanovich's "expressive silence" throughout the second chapter of *The Double*. Standing before the other, the soul does not stand still but constantly lives and dies, hanging at the critical zero point of life and death. Thus, Bakhtin observes, "Dostoevsky always represents a person *on the threshold* of a final decision, at a moment of *crisis*, at an unfinalizable—and *unpredeterminable*—turning point for his soul" (*Problems* 61). Dostoevsky, indeed, often places his character literally at the threshold; think of Golyadkin at the entrance to Olsufy Ivanovich's social gathering and Raskolnikov poised with the axe on the pawnbroker's doorstep in *Crime and Punishment* (*Prestuplenie i nakazanie*). In the polyphonic form characterizing Dostoevsky's art, counterpoint signifies turning point. And being on the threshold means being in the face of the other.

We might therefore question Gide's assertion that Dostoevsky's art "is not the result of observations of the real; or at least, not of that alone. Nor is it the fruit of a preconceived idea, and that is why it is never mere theorizing, but remains steeped in reality. It is the fruit of intercourse between fact and idea" (97). In response to Gide, we should point out first of all that reality is not something we observe "out there"; nor is it a strictly subjective construct. Rather, it arises *between* mind and object, so that the reality Gide speaks of is a product of the interaction between author and world.

"World," moreover, is not a dead datum but a living multitude of voices and consciousnesses, and any notion of "fact" is couched in an idea. It is the face, not fact, that speaks. Levinas may help us with his insight that "the epiphany of that which can present itself directly, outwardly and eminently—is *visage*. The expressing helps the expression here, brings help to itself, signifies, speaks" ("Signature" 185). The stillness of a stone—the silence of the underground man's wall of "nature's laws, the conclusions of natural science, mathematics" (Dostoevsky, *Zapiski* 105)—is not the silence of a face. As Bakhtin puts it, "in stillness nothing makes a sound; in silence no one speaks. Silence is possible only in the human realm" (*Estetika* 338). If one should point out, with Bakhtin, that Raskolnikov, for instance, "does not think about phenomena, he speaks with them" (*Problems* 237), we may answer that he speaks in reply to a voice that summons him from within and from beyond phenomena, the voice of the spirit or truth, if you will, the voice of the one who witnesses every dialogue from a third position. If this is what Gide has in mind, then we see that the intercourse between fact and idea may be the "great dialogue" Bakhtin invokes when he says, "All relationships among external and internal parts and elements of his [Dostoevsky's] novel are dialogic in character, and he structured the novel as a whole as a '*great dialogue*' " (*Problems* 40). The "great dialogue" with whom? With the other, the world, spirit, oneself—both within and beyond the novel.

Dialogical structure and polyphonic form, on Bakhtin's view, are synonymous. "*The polyphonic novel,*" he declares, "*is dialogic through* and *through*"; dialogical relationships, he adds, permeate "all human speech and all relationships and manifestations of human life—in general, everything that has meaning and significance" (*Problems* 40). Polyphonic form is here intrinsic to meaning, which is grounded in a process of listening and response. "I call meaning responses to questions," Bakhtin writes in his "Notes from 1970-1971." "That which responds to no question is, for us, void of meaning"; and meaning "exists only for other meaning, that is, coexists with it" (*Estetika* 350). The polyphony of voice is therefore a polyphony of meaning, a counterposition of question and response. What must be noted in this regard is the importance of the question. The underground man's stone wall is the wall of fixed formulas and ready answers; it is the wall of authoritative reason and syllogistic conclusions; it is, as the underground man suggests, the wall of death (Dostoevsky, *Zapiski* 118-19). Questions break down this wall to make room for dialogue as it unfolds in Dostoevsky's novels. Questions are the life of dialogue; dialogue is the source of meaning; meaning is the substance of life. "To be means to communicate dialogically," observe Clark and Holquist (86). It has been said that when dialogue ends, everything ends. Here let it be added that when the question ends, dialogue ends.

As Berdyaev has noted, Dostoevsky generally plays the dialogical counterposition of question and response off a central position, a central voice, that poses questions and makes responses to other voices. "Dostoevsky's novels," he writes, "are all built up around a central figure, whether the secondary characters converge towards it or the reverse" (*Dostoevsky* 41). We must remind ourselves, however, that this central voice is not the voice of the author's message but the reference point for the interaction of voices. To be sure, it happens, as in the case of Stavrogin in *The Possessed,* that the central figure never actually voices his ideas; instead, we hear only the responses of Shatov, Kirillov, and Verkhovensky to that voice. Their responses, in turn, place Stavrogin in a position of responsibility: the central figure is not a static sounding board but an active respondent. This movement of convergence, this orientation toward the other's voice, is the distinguishing, dynamic feature of polyphonic form.

Bakhtin has understood further that such movement is not simply an aesthetic matter but constitutes the expression of a certain ideological outlook: "A distrust of convictions and their usual monologic function, a quest for truth not as the deduction of one's own consciousness, in fact not in the monologic context of an individual consciousness at all, but rather in the ideal authoritative image of another human being, an orientation toward the other's voice, the other's word: all this is characteristic of Dostoevsky's form-shaping ideology" (*Problems* 98). It is also characteristic of his ideology-shaping form, since, as Bakhtin realizes, "one of the most basic tasks for the novel" is "the laying-bare of conventionality, the exposure of all that is vulgar and falsely stereotyped in human relationships" (*Dialogic* 162). But perhaps *seeking* is a better term than *shaping* in this instance. For the voice of the other is constantly questioning, continually reshaping form and idea. *Notes from Underground* is a good example. The change in form from part one to part two corresponds to a change in the problem facing the underground man: he shifts from the difficulty of being alone—"I am alone, while they are *everyone*" (Dostoevsky, *Zapiski* 125)—to the task of generating a relation with the other, with Liza.

Reading Bakhtin's statements concerning the distrust of conviction and the laying bare of convention, we see more clearly why Gide remarks that "convention is the great breeder of falsehood" (121). When conviction takes the form of automatic answer, it is, like convention, a monological declaration, and not a dialogical interrelation; it is "an avoidance of activity," Clark and Holquist explain, "that has the effect of making my life a subfunction of a self-imposed 'axiological reflex' (*cennostnyj refleks*), similar to Hei-

degger's *das Man*" (76). The monological is untruth. For untruth is
the mimicry of the formula, in which the man is no longer speaking
but is spoken. Recall, for instance, Golyadkin's repeated insertion
of "as they say" in *The Double* (Dostoevsky, *Dvoinik* 119, 120, 121,
125) and his insistence that nevertheless he is his own man (124).
We are reminded in this connection of Lacan's assertion that if a
person can be the slave of language, he "is all the more so of a discourse in the universal movement in which his place is already inscribed at birth, if only by virtue of his proper name" (*Écrits* 148).

Truth happens only where one's voice arises in a contrapuntal
manner, as a response that calls for response. This is what characterizes polyphonic form. We shall go into other implications of
form for a view of truth below. Here let it be noted that a notion of
truth lies beyond polyphonic form and that polyphonic form, in
turn, has ramifications for how we view truth. Recalling in this
connection Berdyaev's statement about the central figure, we
discover that the convergence of one character toward another
constitutes both the formal interaction of voices and the dialogical
quest for truth. One character encounters another not to convert
but to question, as when Ivan confronts Alyosha with the suffering
of the children in *The Brothers Karamazov* (Dostoevsky, *Brat'ya*
262-69). The distrust of conventional convictions, moreover, is
found not only in the orientation toward the other's word, as
distinguished from the discourse of the crowd, but in the form of
the novel itself. Hence Bakhtin contends, "This ability of the novel
to criticize itself is a remarkable feature of this ever-developing
genre" (*Dialogic* 6). Ever-developing, the novel is anticonven-
tional. The dialogical relation between characters engages the
novel in an implied dialogue with itself; turning back on itself, it
participates in its own polyphony.

The more profound the novel's consciousness of itself, the more
pronounced the polyphonic form within the novel. In his study of
Dostoevsky, Berdyaev perceives the tension of polyphony within
the author's works, noting that "a centrifugal and centripetal
movement among human beings runs through all the novels" (44).
Berdyaev's remark immediately brings to mind Bakhtin's view of
language—the basis of human relations—as a composite of centrifugal and centripetal forces. While Dostoevsky's style is a unify-
ing feature of discourse in his novels, the polyphonic form has a

disunifying effect; polyphonic form is made up of heteroglossia—a stratification and opposition of discourses—in tension with the unitary language of style. "This stratification and heteroglossia, once realized," Bakhtin writes, "is not only a static invariant of linguistic life, but also what insures its dynamics: stratification and heteroglossia widen and deepen as long as language is alive and developing. Alongside the centripetal forces, the centrifugal forces of language carry on their uninterrupted work; alongside verbal-ideological centralization and unification, the uninterrupted process of decentralization and disunification go forward" (*Dialogic* 272).

Thus, since they are composed of discourse, the characters in a polyphonic novel develop in the centrifugal and centripetal manner Berdyaev notes. This movement, we must note, is peculiar not only to polyphonic form but to dialogical relation. When the word brings two characters together—in the conversations between Raskolnikov and Porfiry in *Crime and Punishment*, for example—it both announces a union and creates a division, or an alienation, as Lacan might describe it: when a character like Raskolnikov generates his discourse "*for another,* he finds again the fundamental alienation which made him construct it *like another one,* and which has always destined it to be stripped from him *by another*" (*Language* 11). The discourse of one character is at once distinct from and shaped by the discourse of the other. In the action of being drawn together and torn apart, each increases as he is afflicted; both are oriented toward a single referential object, such as Ivan and Alyosha's orientation toward the plight of the children, yet each is simultaneously wounded and made whole by the other's word.

The point that Berdyaev and Bakhtin make about the centrifugal and centripetal forces among characters and in language, therefore, is also a point about the self-consciousness of a given character. Bakhtin makes this clear, bringing out the polyphonic form of consciousness and of the novel, when he says, "The orientation of one person to another person's discourse and consciousness is, in essence, the basic theme of all Dostoevsky's works. The hero's attitude toward himself is inseparably bound up with the attitude of another toward him. His consciousness of self is constantly perceived against the background of the other's consciousness of him—'I for myself' against the background of 'I for another.' Thus the hero's words about himself are structured under the continuous influence of someone else's words about him" (*Problems* 207). With the for-myself played off against the for-another, the I is forever at a threshold between the two, half in shadow, half in light. The I is not an entity but the polyphonic *event* that occurs in the centrifugal and centripetal encounter between two consciousnesses. This is what makes the word a "two-sided act," to use V.N. Voloshinov's term from *Marxism and the Philosophy of Language*: "It is determined equally by *whose* word it is and by *whom* it is for. As a word, it is precisely the product of the *interrelation between speaker and listener*" (*Marksizm* 87).

The interaction with the other's word further underscores the spatial rather than chronological structure characteristic of polyphonic form. As Heidegger expresses it in *Being and Time*, "Dasein is measured according to its spatiality, and is never in the first instance here but there" (*Sein* 107-8). What Bakhtin refers to as " 'I for myself' against the background of 'I for another' " is the activity of response conjoined with the attentiveness of listening. Either the centrifugal or centripetal movement, taken by itself, would mean the explosion or implosion—in any case the disintegration—of the character. Taken together, the two constitute a bridging function: the task of the I is to become a bridge. Perhaps Clark and Holquist can help explain: "The term Bakhtin proposes for this bridging function is 'answerability' (close to Heidegger's *Sorge*, a response to the 'call' or *Ruf* of Being), where the responding aspect of the word, the *otvet* of *otvetstvennost'*, is given its fullest weight. Responsibility is conceived as the action of responding to the world's need, and is accomplished through the activity of the self's responding to its own need for another" (77). It is from this bridging function that polyphonic form arises.

At this juncture we should recall a point made at the outset, namely, that Bakhtin, Berdyaev, and Gide all recognize the idea in Dostoevsky's novels not as a principle for demonstration but as an object of representation. In the words of Berdyaev, "the hero of the *Letters from the Underworld* is an idea, Raskolnikov is an idea, Stavroguin is an idea, Kirilov, Shatov, Verhovensky, Ivan Karamazov—ideas" (*Dostoevsky* 35). A distinguishing feature of polyphonic form is that the I is of a piece with the idea; here too we find a bridging function at work. Hence what was said of the I in the preceding paragraph may be said of the idea. Indeed, Bakhtin says it: "At that point of contact between voice-consciousnesses the idea is born and lives. The idea—as it was *seen* by Dostoevsky the artist—is not a subjective individual-psychological formation with 'permanent resident rights' in a person's head; no, the idea is inter-individual and inter-subjective—the realm of its existence is not individual consciousness but dialogic communion *between* con-sciousnesses. The idea is a *live event*, played out at the point of dialogic meeting between two or several consciousnesses" (*Problems* 88). Polyphonic form is the midwife of the idea. That the idea is born through intersubjective contact underscores the view of the idea as something sought, in a state of development, rather than something found, in a condition of stasis. Once again we see that for polyphonic form, question—the impetus of interaction—is more essential than answer. Once again we find spatiality taking precedence over temporality: the idea is born and lives in a *space between* one consciousness and another as the two engage in di-alogue. Polyphonic form is the form assumed by the living idea.

Because the idea or character lives only through dialogical interaction with another idea or character, both are alive to the extent that they undergo change; and they undergo change in-asmuch as they remain incomplete, unfinalized. In his own way, Gide sees this when he notes, "The chief protagonists he [Dos-toevsky] does not portray, leaving them to limn in their own portrait, never finished, ever changing, in the course of the nar-rative. His principal characters are always in course of formation, never quite emerging from the shadows" (17). The final word that would serve to define the character is forever yet to be uttered. This yet-to-be is the lingering shadow and the ruling time of polyphonic form. It is not by chance that most of Dostoevsky's characters are raw youths in various stages of becoming. What assumes poly-phonic form, then, is constantly in the course of formation and transformation. Here too we see that what is true of the novel is true of the character; what applies to the character applies to the idea. Already our combination of Bakhtin, Berdyaev, and Gide reveals an indissoluble bond between poetics and philosophy in Dostoevsky's literature, and the middle term in the linkage is the character. Like the novel, the character's voice harbors a legion of voices that interact to bring an idea to life.

In the case of Dostoevsky, then, to understand the idea in the novel is to understand the character, and this requires the reader's dialogical interaction with the character. Bakhtin explains, "What is important to Dostoevsky is not how his hero appears in the world but first and foremost how the world appears to his hero, and how the hero appears to himself. . . . What must be discovered and characterized here is not the specific existence of the hero, not his fixed image, but the *sum total of his consciousness and self-consciousness*" (*Problems* 47-48). What must be understood, in other words, is the personality engaged in a process of listening and responding. If Berdyaev is to "display Dostoievsky's spiritual side" (*Dostoevsky* 11) or Gide to get at "Dostoevsky's secret" concerning "the inner life" (15), then they must penetrate the personality of the character. This brings us to the second point in our consideration of these three thinkers and their approach to Dostoevsky.

THE PENETRATION OF PERSONALITY

Gide claims that "the miracle Dostoevsky accomplished consists in this: each of his characters lives . . . by virtue of his own personality" (16). Most of us are teachers, carpenters, accountants, and so on, except when left alone in our rooms; not so with Dostoevsky's characters. They live by their personalities, not by their professions, which is to say, they live by the expression and penetration of their personalities; they live by their ideas, by their discourse, over against the discourse and the conventions of the crowd. "Dostoevsky's hero," Bakhtin tells us, "always seeks to destroy that framework of *other people*'s words about him that might finalize and deaden him" (*Problems* 59). To live by one's own personality is to live in conflict. This tension characterizes the ongoing state of crisis that distinguishes figures such as Raskolnikov, Shatov, and Dmitri Karamazov. Living by virtue of their personalities, these men are constantly deciding something about themselves in the light of one discourse over against another. For Raskolnikov it is the Napoleonic crime as opposed to redemption; for Shatov it is rebellion as opposed to compassion; for Dmitri it is sensuality as opposed to sacrifice. For all three living is a question of forging a personality through responsibility, which is to say, it is a matter of generating and sustaining a voice of one's own by living in a state of continual decisiveness. For these characters, then, everything is yet to be decided: they live in the ongoing possibility of a new birth.

In the penetration of personality, the thing that must be penetrated is the outlook of *das Man*, or the They; the word must be liberated from language, so that the person does not see as the world sees or speak as it demands. Berdyaev perceives this when he says, "According to Dostoievsky, the inmost part of being cannot express itself in the stable conditions of everyday life; it comes to the light of day only in some flare-up in which the fixed and dead forms of an effete society are destroyed" (*Dostoevsky* 43). The voice of the crowd, the script prepared beforehand by others, is a constant threat to the life of the personality; in the case of Golyadkin in *The Double*, it destroys the personality altogether. "*Das Man*," says Heidegger, "is everywhere, yet in such a way that it slips away when Dasein presses for decision. Because, however, *das Man* presents all judging and deciding as its own, it deprives the individual Dasein of responsibility" (*Sein* 127). Overcoming the outlook of the crowd entails a liberation from the fixed forms of the discourse of the crowd, and this always comes *suddenly*, in an outburst—or in a rebirth. "Dostoievsky was the man of underground convulsions," declares Berdyaev; "his element was fire and his mark was movement" (*Dostoevsky* 33). The soul is born to the light of day in the storm and fire of leaving behind all the ready-made categories of existence. What Gide calls "living by personality" Berdyaev regards as living by "the inmost part of being."

This mode of living, of course, has implications not only for the sort of character we deal with but for the nature of the art we encounter in Dostoevsky's novels. Once again, what Berdyaev and Gide address on the level of ideas Bakhtin also approaches in terms of aesthetics: "Self-consciousness, as the *artistic dominant* governing the construction of a character, cannot lie alongside other features of his image; it absorbs these other features into itself as its own material and deprives them of any power to define and finalize the hero" (*Problems* 50). If the characters live according to the penetration of themselves and if the novels are constructed around a set of characters, then all the details of setting, plot, and so on constitute part of the landscape of the characters' self-consciousness. This is how we are to understand Bakhtin's statement that Raskolnikov does not think about phenomena but rather speaks with them (*Problems* 237). For it is by responding to the world that addresses him that the character absorbs the features of the world into himself as part of the stuff of himself. When, for instance, the underground man laments that "there is no getting out of your-self" (Dostoevsky, *Zapiski* 102), he asserts that for him there is no escape from the underground: he is the *underground* man, with all the features of the underground reflected in his self-consciousness. The problem he faces is how to absorb the features of the under-ground in such a way as to deprive the conventions of any power to define him. To the extent that he lives, he cannot be defined because he cannot be confined to convention. The fixed and finalized forms of an effete society are destroyed as they are internalized and transformed, made into aspects of the character's internal life. Thus he is constantly at odds with anything that might settle matters, forever engaged in a dialogue between the internal and the external, between the I-self and the They-self, between what is hidden underground and what is given.

In Dostoevsky's characters, then, there is always something more to come to light. As Bakhtin points out, *"In a human being there is always something that only he himself can reveal, in a free act of self-consciousness and discourse"* (*Problems* 58). That something remains hidden in discourse suggests a certain guilt, and this is why *Crime and Punishment* is not simply a novel about crime but a novel about discourse. In the words of Lacan, "it is the virtue of the *verbe* which perpetuates the movement of the Great Debt" (*Language* 41). The Fall is a fall into language. Here we see the vital importance of confession for figures such as Raskolnikov, Stavrogin, and Ivan Karamazov. If the life of discourse lies in responsibility, then it also lies in confession, for what is confessed is precisely what only I myself can reveal. Gide, in fact, notes this aspect of Dostoevsky's characters, who, he says, "are seized at certain moments—and almost invariably in unexpected and ill-advised fashion—with the urgent desire to make confession, to ask pardon of some fellow-creature who often has not a notion what it is all about" (79). In Dostoevsky's novels the character's present turns on what he has seen and on what he is yet to become; his substance is rooted in a responsibility that belongs to no one else and that is forever yet to be fulfilled. His confession, then, is the "saying" that Levinas describes as "a sign of giving signs, that is, of this non-indifference, a sign of this impossibility of slipping away and being replaced, of this identity, this uniqueness: here I am" (*Otherwise* 145).

Because the character is steeped in responsibility, our vision of him is shaped as much by what we do not see as by what we see; the novels operate according to what is yet to be revealed. Gide makes this point when he asserts, "In Dostoevsky's books, as in a Rembrandt portrait, the shadows are essential. Dostoevsky groups his characters and happenings, plays a brilliant light upon them, illuminating one aspect only. Each of his characters has a deep setting of shadow, reposes on its own shadow almost" (99). The brilliant light is the process of becoming, illuminated through crisis. The shadow is the shadow of the *not yet,* for self-consciousness is consciousness of the *not yet,* of the future perfect of what the character shall have been, in the light of what he is becoming. This aspect of Dostoevsky's characters lies behind Gide's remark that "it seems to be the genesis of feelings that interests him chiefly, for he depicts them [his characters] as indistinct, in their larval state, so to speak" (109). The allusion to shadow and the emphasis on genesis underscore the consciousness of a word yet to be uttered that sustains the character's dialogical movement inward, to the "discovery of the 'man in man,' " as Bakhtin puts it (*Problems* 58). The "man in man" is another expression for what only the character himself can reveal in a movement beyond his "larval state." And he has yet to reveal it even to himself.

Continually living on the threshold of the yet-to-be, the character is constantly at odds with himself. While Berdyaev and Gide see this quite correctly as an existential point about the life of the self, Bakhtin understands it in artistic terms as well: "A man never coincides with himself. One cannot apply to him the formula of identity A = A. In Dostoevsky's artistic thinking, the genuine life of the personality takes place at the point of non-coincidence between a man and himself, at his point of departure beyond the limits of all that he is as a material being, a being that can be spied on, defined, predicted apart from its own will, 'at second hand.' The genuine life of the personality is made available only through a *dialogic* penetration of that personality" (*Problems* 59). Bakhtin's statement rings of the alogical, existential assertion that a person is what he is not and is not what he is. The penetration of personality is not a matter of logic but of dialogic. Logic does its work without the man; it is not by virtue of my resolve or response that a syllogism is true or false. The genuine life of the personality emerges only where there is human relation grounded in a process of hearing and responding. Dostoevsky's characters are engaged in action even when they are doing nothing. One striking example of this movement at the spot may be found in Kirillov from *The Possessed*, who, it seems, never leaves his room, yet is central to the action of the novel. It is important to bear in mind, then, that the self is not precisely the personality but the *event* of the dialogical penetration of the personality. The self is not an entity but a force or the locus of a force, never here but always elsewhere, living according to a principle of uncertainty. It is equally important to note that the event that is the self is something willed and not something imposed, "at second hand." The penetration of personality must be undertaken by the personality itself. The free act of self-consciousness Bakhtin refers to above is an act of self-will.

The question that arises in this connection is whether the self-will or the resolve of the personality is grounded in a higher, spiritual relation—that is, in a dialogical relation—or is left to an arbitrary void. "That," says Berdyaev, "is what interested Dostoievsky: what happens to man when, having liberty, he must needs turn aside to arbitrary self-will" (*Dostoevsky* 46). In Kirillov, of course, we see the void of self-will when it is not grounded in anything outside itself. "If there is a God," he tells Verkhovensky, "then everything is His will, and I cannot escape His will. If not, then everything is my will, and I am bound to show self-will" (Dostoevsky, *Besy* 641). Further on Kirillov states the problem before us in even stronger terms: "The attribute of my divinity is self-will! In this alone can I prove at the highest point my independence and my terrible new freedom. For it is very terrible. I am killing myself to demonstrate my independence and my terrible new freedom" (644). We see something similar, though not as eloquent, in another one of Dostoevsky's suicides—Smerdyakov of *The Brothers Karamazov.* Lacan's comment on human liberty in *The Language of the Self* perfectly describes both characters: "Man's liberty is entirely inscribed within the constituting triangle of the renunciation which he imposes on the desire of the other by the menace of death for the *jouissance* of the fruits of his serfdom—of the consented-to sacrifice of his life for the reasons which give human life its measure—and of the suicidal renouncement of the vanquished partner, balking of his victory the master whom he abandons to his inhuman solitude" (84).

In the tension surrounding freedom and self-will lies the great danger, something that the Grand Inquisitor understands very well and that Berdyaev sees lurking in the shadows so essential to Dostoevsky's characters: "Human freedom abandoned the psychic world in whose daylight it had existed since the Renaissance and plunged into the depths of the spiritual world. It is like a descent into Hell. But there man will find again not only Satan and his kingdom, but also God and Heaven; and they will no longer be revealed in accordance with an objective order imposed from without but by way of a face-to-face meeting with the ultimate depths of the human spirit, as an inwardly revealed reality. All Dostoievsky's work is an illustration of this" (*Dostoevsky* 49). In Heidegger's words, "freedom" is indeed "the abyss of Dasein" (*Essence* 129).

Whether or not we challenge Berdyaev's assertion that since the Renaissance freedom had been couched in the "psychic world," there is in Dostoevsky a plunge into the depths—or an ascent into the heights—of the spiritual world, which is the world of the dialogical word. The objective order Berdyaev cites is the order of the monological word; the face-to-face meeting is the place of dialogue. The penetration of the "ultimate depths of the human spirit" always occurs before the face. Why? Because, as Levinas explains it, "the face is signification, and signification without context. . . . The face is meaning all by itself. You are you. In this sense one can say that the face is not 'seen.' It is what cannot become a content, which your thought would embrace; it is uncontainable, it leads you beyond" (*Ethics* 86-87). Thus in Dostoevsky the inward reality, the beyond, is revealed in such face-to-face encounters as those between Raskolnikov and Sonya in *Crime and Punishment*, Myshkin and Ippolit in *The Idiot*, Christ and the Grand Inquisitor in *The Brothers Karamazov*. For Dostoevsky, the other is not a limitation on freedom but the doorway to freedom, since the other is the portal to the idea as it lives in dialogical interaction. "For Dostoievsky," says Berdyaev, "the theme of man and his destiny is in the first place the theme of freedom, . . . freedom is the centre of his conception of the world, . . . his hidden pathos is a pathos of freedom" (*Dostoevsky* 67). This statement reminds us of Clark and Holquist's observation that Bakhtin was above all "a philosopher of freedom" (11).

If what Bakhtin says is true, that "only the unfinalized and inexhaustible 'man in man' can become a man of the idea" (*Problems* 86), it is because the "man in man" is the man in collision with freedom and self-will in the spiritual depths that Berdyaev describes. One will recall the assertion in *Notes from Underground* that the will is an expression of the whole of human life (Dostoevsky, *Zapiski* 115), anticipating Heidegger's remark that "every being, as a being, is in the will" (*Poetry* 100). Yet the will that distinguishes the personality and gives life to the idea threatens the freedom that allows the penetration of personality. The "man in man" comes to light in this conflict; the man of the idea is born from these extremes. For the idea is made of the dialogical tension between freedom and self-will, between the Madonna and Sodom, as Dmitri Karamazov expresses it (Dostoevky, *Brat'ya* 120-21).

In the novel this tension unfolds in the word when, in the language of Voloshinov, "*the word is not an expression of inner personality, but rather inner personality is the expressed or impelled word*" (*Marksizm* 151). As the constitutive feature of the personality, the idea, which is the artistic dominant in Dostoevsy's novels, is both the product of and the pathway to the spirit. The spirit lies unfinalized on the other side of the penetration of the personality; it is the thing forever yet to be penetrated, and it underlies both the idea and the art. What is formative of the character is formative of the novel; a poetics of spirit is a poetics of personality and affects both the man on the page and the man before the page—and within each the "man in man," the man as will and idea. We must be careful to note in this connection, as Bakhtin does, that "personalization is in no sense subjectivization. The limit here is not *I* but *I* within a relationship to other personalities, that is, *I* and the *other*, *I* and *Thou*" (*Estetika* 370). Conceived dialogically, for the sake of the relation between I and the other, will and idea forge the tools for the constitution and penetration of personality. Isolated from the relation to the other, however, they pose the greatest of threats to the life of the personality. Instead of forming the soil from which the "man in man" may grow, will and idea become the grave in which the man is buried. Hence Dmitri Karamazov's assertion that Ivan is a tomb (Dostoevsky, *Brat'ya* 123).

Opposite the dialogical penetration of personality, by which the character lives spiritually, is the monological self-affirmation of personality, by which he dies spiritually; this death is what dialogue sets out to overcome. In the case of Ivan Karamazov, his conversations with Alyosha in the chapters "Over Brandy" and "Rebellion" are not simply challenges and self-justifications but are also outcries for the response from his brother that might give him life. In offering Alyosha his prose poem "The Grand Inquisitor," Ivan does not so much seek the last word as a response. And he receives just that: a kiss that is beyond words. Ivan is thus thrown back on himself to work out, in dialogue with himself, the very problem of freedom that his Grand Inquisitor pretends to resolve. Thus freedom is opposed to necessity and decisiveness to the impotence to choose. Freedom in this case does not lie in having but in offering; it is not freedom from but freedom for and responsibility to the other. In Dostoevsky's novels compulsion is most terrible when it assumes the guise of caprice. "Once man has set his foot upon the road of self-will and self-affirmation," Berdyaev points out, "he must sacrifice the primacy of spirit and his original freedom and become the plaything of necessity and compulsion" (*Dostoevsky* 82). As Gide states it, "in Dostoevsky's novels, the *will to power* leads inevitably to ruin" (88). It is important to remember, however, that even self-will is here to be understood in terms of a relation to the other; as Lacan has said, "the first object of desire is to be recognized by the other" (*Language* 31). In *Notes from Underground* self-will or the will to power finds its expression in the underground man's declaration that the world can go to the devil as long as he has his tea (Dostoevsky, *Zapiski* 174); in *The Brothers Karamazov* we hear it in Ivan's insistence on his own burning indignation over injustice, even if he were wrong (*Brat'ya* 268-69).

At the end of the road cited by Berdyaev and Gide lies murder, as in the case of Raskolnikov, or suicide, as in the case of Kirillov. Once again we see that spiritual death comes with monological isolation, while spiritual life revolves around dialogical penetration. This life-and-death theme runs throughout Dostoevsky's works, so that we cannot help but question Clark and Holquist's claim that Dostoevsky is "utterly uninterested in death" (246). Losing contact with the word of the other, which is indispensable to dialogue, the character reaches a position where he cannot do other than what the monological voice requires; thus becoming the plaything of compulsion, he dies in one form or another. The I-for-myself loses the I-for-the-other, loses the dialogical relation, and finally loses itself. The monological idea speaks for the self and dictates to it, so that the self is lost and the man cannot speak at all. Think of Kirillov in his last hour of life, paralyzed and struck dumb. Failing to live dialogically, the individual fails to live decisively, as Berdyaev points out in regard to Stavrogin: "Good and evil, our Lady and Sodom, were equally attractive to Stavroguin, and this inability to make a choice is the exact indication of the alienation of freedom and loss of personality that are involved in self-will and inner division" (*Dostoevsky* 125). In the life of the personality, monologue divides, while dialogue makes whole; monologue enslaves, while dialogue liberates, and only in liberty does the personality live. Whereas in monologue the ideological principle eclipses the man's relation to the other, in dialogue he is continually penetrating himself through his relation to the other. In that relation he must gather himself to respond as he is summoned, and nothing he might have prepared beforehand can take the place of his response. The character cannot "cookbook" his way through the situation that confronts him any more than the critic can "cookbook" his way through the text. Every context calls for my presence, my responsibility, my voice.

The inner division Berdyaev alludes to comes with a muting of the voice, with the inability to respond. As Bakhtin has observed, this point is especially pronounced in Golyadkin from *The Double*, a character whose "speech seeks, above all, to simulate total independence from the other's word" (*Problems* 217-18); failing to respond to the other's word, Golyadkin ends up losing his own word. Hence, instead of a penetration of the personality, we have a splitting of the personality. As Lacan states it in *The Language of the Self*, "the absence of the Word is manifested here by the stereotypes of a discourse in which the subject, one might say, is spoken rather than speaking" (43). When the subject is "spoken" by the other, he is made other to himself and is thus torn from himself. One way in which this comes out in *The Double* is through Golyadkin's repeated use of proverbs and popular phrases. One will note further that Golyadkin is often tongue-tied and has trouble getting his words out at all, even to the point of a virtual paralysis of voice (for example, Dostoevsky, *Dvoinik* 112, 124, 133-34). And he is never so irrevocably in the grips of the other as when he shrinks into panicked flight upon encountering a colleague or ranking superior (for example, 112, 113). Once more, the splitting of the personality—in contrast to the penetration of the personality—occurs when the relation of dialogue with the other is displaced by the nonrelation of dominance by the other.

While the theme of doubling goes to its extreme in *The Double*, it turns up in most of the novels; Ivan Karamazov's conversation with the devil readily comes to mind. Gide has noted the importance—and the threat—of the dual self in the penetration of personality (103), but Bakhtin brings out its significance both for the character and for the novel: "At the heart of the genre lies the discovery of the *inner man*—'one's own self,' accessible not to passive self-observation but only through an *active dialogic approach to one's own self,* destroying the naive wholeness of one's notions about the self that lies at the heart of the lyric, epic, and tragic image of men. A dialogic approach to oneself breaks down the outer shell of the self's image, that shell which exists for other people, determining the external assessment of a person (in the eyes of others) and dimming the purity of self-consciousness" (*Problems* 120). We have seen how, for Golyadkin, the outer shell creates division; here Bakhtin argues that such division is overcome through dialogical penetration of the self. The novel itself is a penetration of the self; the novel always entails a concept of a hidden self. Here lies a crucial connection between poetics and theme: constructed according to the tension between voices, the novel always deals with the problem of self and other. Bakhtin's statement reminds us once more of how, in Berdyaev's words, "the fixed and dead forms of an effete society are destroyed" (*Dostoevsky* 43). Among those forms is the outer shell of the self's image. For an example of the outer shell at work, recall the "noble expression" that the underground man assumes upon entering his office (Dostoevsky, *Zapiski* 124) or his assertion that he hates his face yet takes pleasure in looking repulsive to others (151).

We see, then, the wrongheadedness of Gide's statement that for Dostoevsky "the inner life is more highly prized than relations to one's fellow-man" (15). There is no "inner life" apart from the relation to one's fellowman. In the dialogical penetration of personality, self-consciousness is mediated by a dialogical relation to the other; the way of active dialogical approach to oneself is the way of response to the other, not to the They but to the Thou. Says Bakhtin, "Only in communion, in the interaction of one person with another, can the 'man in man' be revealed, for others as well as for oneself" (*Problems* 252); this statement echoes Heidegger's assertion that "selfhood is the presupposition of the possibility of being an 'I', which itself is revealed only in the Thou" (*Essence* 87). It is on this threshold, in a space *between,* that spiritual life opens up.

Thus we discover in Dostoevsky—both in the ideas and in the poetics—that the barriers to the penetration of personality are those that isolate the self from the other; whether it is by the monologue of self-will or by the mimicry of *das Man,* the self is imprisoned all the same, confined to the finitude and therefore to the nothingness of itself. Selfhood is freedom, and freedom is attained only in the dialogical encounter between the I and the other, which transforms both. It is what Levinas calls "the psyche" when he says, "I exist through the other and for the other, but without this being alienation: I am inspired. This inspiration is the psyche" (*Otherwise* 114). Because every encounter entails transformation, the freedom found there signifies the infinite. As Berdyaev puts it, "freedom sets itself up against the exclusive domination of the formal element and the building of barriers; it presupposes the infinite" (*Dostoevsky* 73-74). Presupposing the infinite, it presupposes the spirit, or at least a living bond between spirit and personality. Freedom penetrates the barriers in a penetration of personality through the word, suggesting that the word must be viewed in terms of spirit. But since freedom entails the offering of the self to and for the other, whereby the self is transfigured, the penetration of personality is ultimately accomplished in a renunciation of personality. Indeed, the spirit appropriates through renunciation: those who surrender their lives receive life.

In the provocative words of Bakhtin, "the soul is the gift of my spirit to the other" (*Estetika* 116). The soul comes to life as it is offered to the other; this is what it means to live in the spirit.

One thinks of Dmitri Karamazov's decision to sacrifice himself for the babe (Dostoevsky, *Brat'ya* 639) when one hears Gide saying, "Here is the mysterious essence of Dostoevsky's philosophy and of Christian ethics too; the divine secret of happiness. The individual triumphs by renunciation of his individuality. He who lives his life, cherishing personality, shall lose it: but he who surrenders it shall gain the fullness of life eternal, not in the future, but in the present made one with eternity" (130). Remember what Kirillov says in *The Possessed:* "When all men attain happiness, there will be no more time, for it will be unnecessary" (Dostoevsky, *Besy* 251). Time is unhappiness, and unhappiness is the absence of self resulting from the loss of relation to the other. Berdyaev makes a similar remark in *The Destiny of Man* when he says, "Paradise is not in the future, is not in time, but in eternity. Eternity is attained in the actual moment, it comes in the present" (288). How is eternity attained in the present? By penetrating one's personality in the sacrifice of self-serving individuality for the sake of the other. This is how love brings salvation, as Zosima declares in *The Brothers Karamazov* (Dostoevsky, *Brat'ya* 62). Like Gide, Berdyaev attempts to give utterance to the divine secret in what may be regarded as a free translation of Gide's insight: "Personality is bound up with love, but it is a love that goes out towards fellowship with another human being" (*Dostoevsky* 126). The literary form that concerns Bakhtin harbors the truth that is revealed to Berdyaev and Gide. It is a truth that summons the language of freedom and infinity, of love and eternity. In short, it is spiritual truth.

SPIRITUAL TRUTH

While Bakhtin is clearly occupied with aesthetic form, as suggested above, he, like Berdyaev and Gide, is also involved with spiritual truth. This involvement is most evident in his *Aesthetics of Verbal Art*, where he states, "Wherever the alibi becomes a prerequisite for creation and expression there can be no responsibility, no seriousness, no meaning. A special responsibility is required . . . ; but this responsibility can be founded only on a profound belief in a higher truth, . . . the belief that another, higher being responds to my special responsibility, that I do not act in an utter void. Apart from this belief there can be only empty pretense" (*Estetika* 179). The sort of alibi Bakhtin has in mind may be writing strictly for the sake of publication, promotion, or various forms of profit—in short, writing for the marketplace. Literature cannot be literature if it becomes a commodity for consumption. "As language becomes more functional," Lacan has noted, "it becomes improper for the Word" (*Language* 62); as literature becomes more functional, it becomes improper for the spirit, improper for truth, and fails to meet the special responsibility. If literature has a function, it is to affirm and bear witness to the responsibility it meets "in a perpetual return upon itself," as Foucault expresses it; "it addresses itself to itself as a writing subjectivity, or seeks to re-apprehend the essence of all literature in the movement that brought it into being" (*Order* 300). And the essence of literature is the special responsibility Bakhtin invokes.

Berdyaev and Gide would, no doubt, agree with Bakhtin's position. Berdyaev, in fact, makes a similar claim: "If all things are allowable to man, then freedom becomes its own slave, and the man who is his own slave is lost. The human image needs the support of a higher nature, and human freedom reaches its definitive expression in a higher freedom, freedom in truth. The dialectic is irrefutable. And it draws us into the wake of God-made-man, by whom alone human freedom can be joined with divine freedom and the form of man with the form of God" (*Dostoevsky* 76). Here one understands that self-will is the lie opposed by spiritual truth. The higher freedom in truth is born in the higher responsibility to truth. Responsibility is the key: to know what spiritual truth entails is to know what responsibility entails. It is a matter between one and the other, the offering of one's word and one's self to and for the sake of the other. To be capable of response is to be capable of hearing the summons to respond that comes from the other and from beyond him. As we speak, we hear, bearing witness to the truth for the sake of the truth as expressed in the I-for-the-other relation. The import of the testimony lies not so much in its content as in what happens to the witness as he speaks. Recall, for example, Dostoevsky's ridiculous man, who speaks his truth for the sake of the little girl that first summoned and then saved him.

Where is the "higher truth" revealed? In the tears of a child weeping for her mother.

We must be quick to point out that the dialectic Berdyaev cites above is not to be confused with the Hegelian dialectic Bakhtin refers to when he says, "The unified, dialectically evolving spirit, understood in Hegelian terms, can give rise to nothing but a philosophical monologue" (*Problems* 26). One thinks of Dostoevsky's assertion in *The Unpublished Dostoevsky* that "through faithfulness to poetic truth incomparably more of our history can be conveyed than through faithfulness *only* to history" (*Neizdannyi* 613). For poetic truth is spiritual truth. In Dostoevsky's poetics the spirit does not evolve—it devolves, living in the transfer from mouth to ear, from eye to eye. Although it may be linked with an evolution of ideas, it does not dissolve into that evolution. Berdyaev's dialectic does not pertain to an evolving spirit but to a transformation of the individual in the face of a spiritual truth that is forever finished but never fulfilled. It addresses not a universal system but the single person. It rests not on a monological principle but on a dialogical process. The dialectic in this instance, like the structure of the novels, is spatial rather than temporal, existential rather than historical. It is not so much a movement *from* the spot as a movement *at* the spot.

Berdyaev describes the dialectic he has in mind by saying, "Free goodness involves the freedom of evil; but freedom of evil leads to the destruction of freedom itself and degeneration into an evil necessity. On the other hand, the denial of the freedom of evil in favour of an exclusive freedom of good ends equally in a negation of freedom and its degeneration—into a good necessity. But a good necessity is not good, because goodness resides in freedom from necessity" (*Dostoevsky* 70). The freedom and goodness Berdyaev refers to revolve around the "special responsibility" discussed earlier; instead of slipping into a "good necessity," the individual faces the impossibility of escaping his responsibility. I cannot withhold meaning, and this, as Clark and Holquist point out, "constitutes a responsibility: I am answerable in the sense that I am free to heed or ignore the world's call for a response" (76); that is, I can choose to heed or choose to ignore, but I cannot choose not to choose. Freedom from the evil necessity rests on freedom in the truth. To be free from necessity is to be free for response: freedom is responsibility, is the ability to respond. In responsive interaction, then, the dialectic of the "good necessity" and the "evil necessity" is worked out. Although he is confined to a cell, Dmitri Karamazov finds freedom in his responsibility for the babe; whatever the sentence pronounced upon him, he will go not by necessity but by choice, in responsibility. Yet, at the same time, he cannot do otherwise.

If responsibility is the key to spiritual truth, moreover, it is the mainstay of dialogue; there can be no dialogue without response, and spiritual truth is dialogical truth. Once more, Bakhtin understands that what applies to the theme of Dostoevsky's novels also applies to the genre itself, with the poetics of the art resting on a concept of truth: "At the base of the genre lies the Socratic notion of the dialogic nature of truth, and the dialogic nature of human thinking about truth. The dialogic means of seeking truth is counterposed to *official* monologism, which pretends to *possess a ready-made truth.* . . . Truth is not born nor is it to be found inside the head of an individual person, it is born *between people* collectively searching for truth, in the process of their dialogic interaction" (*Problems* 110). *Seeking* here stands over against *possessing.* Truth is not whatever is the case, not a datum, but an *event* that takes place between two or more voices. Truth is a verb. It sets us free by setting us in motion, in the movement of question and quest opposite the stasis of the found and the rigor mortis of the ready-made. The spirit is a question mark, not an exclamation point. A distinguishing feature of spiritual truth is that it lies more in the seeking than in the finding, more in the questions than in the conclusions. To be sure, the process of raising and responding to questions characterizes dialogical interaction; even assertions, if they are dialogical, harbor a question. Again, when the questions come to an end, so does the dialogue—so does the relation to truth and the life of the self. Nothing is more deadly to the spirit than a ready-made answer.

We can see that Gide has a sense of what Bakhtin asserts when we read, "The ideas he [Dostoevsky] submits are most often left in the problematic state, in the form of a question. He is seeking not so much a solution as an exposition of these very questions which, by reason of their complexity, confusion, and interdependence, are as a rule left ill-defined" (92). *Exploration* would be a better word than *exposition*, and in Dostoevsky it is pursued both in form and in substance. What is well defined is formally confined, like the self in the shell of its social image. Spiritual truth resides in the open-endedness of the ill defined, in the penetration of form; although it is eternally abiding, it belongs to the word yet to be uttered, to the revelation yet to come. Characterized by interrogative interaction, it is both unsettled and unsettling. Thus Bakhtin quotes *The Notebooks of F.M. Dostoevsky* (179) saying, " 'Reality in its entirety,' Dostoevsky himself wrote, 'is not to be exhausted by what is immediately at hand, for an overwhelming part of this reality is contained in the form of a still *latent, unuttered future Word*" (*Problems* 90). To regard the word as a vessel of reality is to view the word as spirit. In place of "reality in its entirety," then, we may read "spiritual truth," given Bakhtin's definition of the spirit as "the totality of all meaningful significance and direction in life" (*Estetika* 98). To conceptualize the spirit in terms of totality is to treat it not only as a oneness but as an openness or an open-endedness. For the spirit, all things are possible; if a poetics of spirit is a poetics of possibility, then it is a poetics of futurity. The novel is always more prophetic than mimetic—not because it predicts some finality in the future but because it reveals the open-endedness of the present.

Something of the totality is forever yet to unfold, and this is where Dostoevsky places his accent; as Berdyaev puts it, "Dostoevsky is concerned only with that which is to be" (*Dostoevsky* 23). Bakhtin voices the same insight when he declares, "The catharsis that finalizes Dostoevsky's novels might be . . . expressed in this way: *nothing conclusive has yet taken place in the world, the ultimate word of the world and about the world has not yet been spoken, the world is open and free, everything is still in the future and will always be in the future*" (*Problems* 166). In all the ages of humanity there is always someone who insists that the last judgment is at hand, and he is always right. If spiritual truth is dialogical, it is also future-oriented; it knows nothing of the ineluctable past but dwells on the open horizon of possibility that constitutes the future. Or better: it lives in the instant that is the portal to the future, receding even as it is approached. For spiritual truth announces itself as what we fall short of; rooted in responsibility, spiritual truth reveals itself in the response we have yet to make. "The subject is the more responsible the more it answers for," in the words of Levinas, "as though the distance between it and the other increased in the measure that proximity was increased" (*Otherwise* 139-40). Encountering spiritual truth, I always encounter myself as the one who is in error. This is the difficulty facing Dostoevsky's characters; this is what lies behind Alyosha Karamazov's constant confession.

Spiritual truth dwells in the dialogue between two voices, and what Bakhtin says about the life of the word may also be said about the life of the spirit and its truth: "For the word is not a material thing but rather the eternally mobile, eternally fickle medium of dialogic interaction. It never gravitates toward a single consciousness or a single voice. The life of the word is contained in its transfer from one mouth to another, from one context to another context" (*Problems* 202). Just as the word does not sleep within us but rather we live in the word, spiritual truth is not something we discover but is the force and the presence through which we live. The spirit moves where it lists; it draws rather than gravitates, as one would draw a breath. Like the word, spiritual truth abides neither here nor there but *in transfer*, vibrating in the *between*, wherever two are gathered in its name. "Two voices is the minimum for life, the minimum for existence," says Bakhtin (*Problems* 252), because they are the minimum for spiritual presence, for spiritual truth. And two voices is the minimum for the novel, since its poetics is a poetics of spirit. The novel lies in the transfer from hand to page, from page to eye. To the extent that it addresses spiritual truth, the novel is not a material thing but an event, a force, a living voice replete with a legion of voices. "The text as such never appears as a dead thing," Bakhtin insists. "Beginning with any text, we always arrive . . . at the human voice, which is to say we come up against the human being" (*Dialogic* 252-53). When we come up against the human being, we come up against ourselves: touching, we are touched and are thus brought to the threshold.

Since spiritual truth abides in the transfer over the threshold of the between, it lies more in the act of saying than in the said; a poetics of spirit is a poetics of saying, a poetics of process. This threshold of saying is the critical zero point of what is about to be uttered but is *not yet* spoken. There the silence of the passion that moves us to speak can be heard; there it is possible for silence to speak and for the truth to speak in silence. One is reminded of Heidegger's remark that "the call speaks in the uncanny mode of silence" (*Sein* 277). If, as Bakhtin has said, "silence is possible only in the human realm" (*Estetika* 338), it is because the human realm is the realm of dialogue and therefore of spiritual truth. Dealing with process rather than theme, with interaction rather than exposition, Dostoevsky makes silence itself into a character and a witness of spiritual truth, as in the example of Christ before the Grand Inquisitor. Here spiritual truth resounds as a silence without becoming a theme; it is a "preoriginary saying," as Levinas expresses it when he says, "In my giving of signs, already the infinite speaks through the witness I bear of it, in my sincerity, in my saying without said, preoriginary saying which is said in the mouth of the very one that receives the witness" (*Otherwise* 151). "Preoriginary saying" lies in the silence of the word before it is uttered, in the response to the call before it is heard. What Levinas refers to as the infinite we may associate with spiritual truth, which speaks silently through the saying of themes and narratives. While those themes are found "in an atmosphere of the already spoken," to borrow a statement from Bakhtin, "the word is at the same time determined by that which has not been said but which is needed" (*Dialogic* 280). Viewing the spirit as word thus enables us to view the word as a silence, as something that bespeaks what is needful. Hence the truth may speak in silence.

The relationship between silence and spiritual truth comes out more clearly in Berdyaev's comments on Christ and the Grand Inquisitor. He points out, for example, that "Christ is a shadowy figure who says nothing all the time: efficacious religion does not explain itself, the principle of freedom cannot be expressed in words"; and he adds that the Grand Inquisitor "argues and persuades; he is a master of logic and he is single-mindedly set on the carrying-out of a definite plan: but our Lord's silence is stronger and more convincing" (*Dostoevsky* 189). By now we can see that Gide's statement that something of Dostoevsky's characters remains in the shadows (17) is more than an observation about aesthetics: it is an assertion about the relation between silence and spiritual truth. Dostoevsky's characters are incomplete, constantly in a process of formation, because they live in the tension between revelatory word and intractable silence. Dmitri Karamazov's longing for a union with the earth (Dostoevsky, *Brat'ya* 110), for instance, is a longing for the truth that speaks from the silence of the earth, for the preoriginary saying. This condition of incompletion is, indeed, what makes Dmitri a character, unlike Christ in Ivan's prose poem. Clark and Holquist have a helpful insight in this regard: "What is important about Dostoevsky's Christ is the life model he provides, a kind of ideal other; to prefer to err while remaining with Christ is to choose to be without truth in any absolute or even theoretical sense, to give up truth as a formula or truth as a proposition" (248). It is to pursue truth as spirit. Christ here is the ultimate Word, who speaks through his silence, making silence into a dialogical response. In silence, he listens and responds simultaneously; his is the might of the dew, not of the typhoon.

It is also significant that Christ—the one who offers the gift and the burden of responsibility and freedom, who is known as the Word—offers no response, or rather makes silence into a response. Because spiritual truth is dialogical, it does not explain or justify itself; on the contrary, it is the thing by which the dialogue of life with life is justified. Responding to the Grand Inquisitor with silence, Christ responds both from the position of the Thou and from the position of the Third, what Bakhtin terms "the overman, the over-*I*—that is, the [silent] witness and judge of every man (of every *I*)" (*Estetika* 342). To be sure, he is there, between or above Ivan and Alyosha, as a witness to their dialogue; and he is there as a witness to the interaction between reader and text. As the embodiment of spiritual truth, Dostoevsky's Christ is the one who summons every I and Thou to responsive, dialogical relation. What Berdyaev refers to as the logic and single-mindedness of the Grand Inquisitor, on the other hand, is the single-voicedness of monological explanation and self-justification, which seeks not a responsive word but the last word. In the place of freedom he offers a formula, in the place of dialogue a dogma. He is the euclidean in whose world, Berdyaev tells us, "there will be no suffering or responsibility—or freedom either" (*Dostoevsky* 191). Or life, we might add. For the euclidean's world is the monological world of form emptied of substance, of the letter drained of spirit, and of word exiled from meaning.

Berdyaev notes a linkage between suffering and responsibility that is important to an understanding of spiritual truth. Responsibility requires openness and exposure to the other; it requires, in other words, vulnerability to and suffering for the other. The person who offers his word and self to the other offers his face to the other, as one would turn the other cheek to the smiter. For the face speaks, as we have already said, and the exposure of the face bespeaks the openness and vulnerability constituting the dialogical relation wherein spiritual truth dwells. The novel that addresses such truth is just such a face, and its open-endedness is the exposure of a wound: a poetics of spirit is a poetics of the face in its exposure to wounds. It is this concern of the novel that, as Berdyaev notes, "forbids the arbitrary killing of the least and most harmful of men: it means the loss of one's essential humanity and the dissolution of personality" (*Dostoevsky* 97). Hence murder is a frequent focal point for Dostoevsky. The spiritual truth that speaks from the trace of the divine image in the human face forbids us to kill. Once again Levinas's claim that the face is signification without context and that it "leads you beyond" (*Ethics* 86-87) comes to mind. It leads you toward the responsibility of spiritual truth. Responsible for the other to the point of suffering and sacrifice for the other, we are responsible for the life and death of the other. If, in Berdyaev's words, "suffering is an index of man's depth" (*Dostoevsky* 92), it is because suffering is an index of man's responsibility and hence of his relation to spiritual truth. Living in that relation, we learn to declare not "I suffer therefore I am" but "I suffer therefore you are." Here lies the basis of Dostoevsky's poetics of spirit.

Finally, we must note once again that there is a relation between philosophical position and generic form in Dostoevsky's novels. The openness to suffering is connected to the open-endedness of the dialogical relation; and the open-endedness of that relation is linked to the unfinalized form of the novel itself. Clark and Holquist bring out this connection quite well in their discussion of Dostoevsky's Christ: "Dostoevsky is rather a Christ to his characters, like the Christ in *The Brothers Karamazov*: a loving deity, who is silent so that others may speak and, in speaking, enact their freedom. In the best kenotic tradition, Dostoevsky gives up the privilege of a distinct and higher being to descend into his text, to be among his creatures. Dostoevsky's distinctive image of Christ results in the central role of polyphony in his fiction" (249). The message is couched in the form as well as in the content. And with the message there is a summons that is a question. Bakhtin can help in this regard: "Thus Dostoevsky's works contain no final, finalizing discourse that defines anything once and for ever. Thus there can be no firm image of the hero answering to the question 'Who is *he*?' The only questions here are 'Who am *I*?' and 'Who are *you*?' But even these questions reverberate in a continuous and open-ended interior dialogue. Discourse of the hero and discourse about the hero are determined by an open dialogic attitude toward oneself and toward the other" (*Problems* 251).

When Kirillov shouts to Verkhovensky, "Answer, if you're a man!" (Dostoevsky, *Besy* 643), or when Ivan asks Alyosha, "But what am I to do about the children?" (Dostoevsky, *Brat'ya* 267), those questions are also put to you and to me. We cannot deal with spiritual truth unless we deal with ourselves, unless we put the needful questions to ourselves, whether we are concerned with poetics or ideas. Our relation to Dostoevsky's novels has a bearing on our relation to the other, to the human being now before us; and the relation to the other, in turn, influences our relation to the text. "To see and understand an author's work," Bakhtin once wrote, "is to see and understand another, alien consciousness and its world, that is, another subject ('Du')" (*Estetika* 289). We cannot treat the literary text as an object of academic curiosity but must respond to it as a living voice, if we are to receive the message lying in its generic features as well as in its thematic development. As Bakhtin, Berdyaev, and Gide have shown us in their own response to Dostoevsky, when we answer to the truth of the literature we also answer to spiritual truth.

If there is one concept, one word, that ties together polyphonic form, the penetration of personality, and spiritual truth, it is *transformation*. In the foregoing we have seen that the fixed forms of convention are transformed in polyphony; that the penetration of personality begets a transformation of personality; and that spiritual truth is born in a dialogical encounter, which changes each member of the encounter. The notion of transformation, of rebirth and resurrection, moreover, is one that joins Bakhtin, Berdyaev, and Gide with respect to the general scope of their approaches to Dostoevsky. Gide, for example, cites three "strata or regions" that he distinguishes in the characters of Dostoevsky's novels. The first, he tells us, is the intellectual, and the second is the region of passion. But, says Gide, "there is a region deeper still, where passion exists not. This is the region that resurrection . . . enables us to reach as Raskolnikov reached it" (114). Similarly, and especially in his remarks about Alyosha Karamazov, Berdyaev emphasizes the "dazzling truth of the religion of resurrection" (*Dostoevsky* 207) that reveals itself in Dostoevsky's works. Both Berdyaev and Gide, then, testify to the truth of Bakhtin's assertion that "I live in the depths of myself through faith and hope in the ongoing possibility of the inner miracle of a new birth" (*Estetika* 112).

As different as these three figures are in their treatment of Dostoevsky, they all show us that we cannot understand Dostoevsky without being undone. What served as an epigram to his last novel may also serve as a closing remark to this comparison of Bakhtin, Berdyaev, and Gide: "Verily, verily, I say unto you, Except a kernel of wheat fall to the earth and die, it abides alone: but if it dies, it brings forth much fruit" (John 12:24). Although we have traveled a different route, we find in this notion of rebirth a point of intersection with the remarks on literature and creation in the first essay.

By now it should be clear that a poetics of spirit entails a concept of self and bears implications for the relation between the author's creation of a character and the human being's creation of a self. To be sure, Clark and Holquist have noted that "although the self/other is a recurring preoccupation of many other post-Romantic systems of thought, Bakhtin is the only major figure to form the problem in terms of authorship. He is distinguished not by his emphasis on the self/other dichotomy as such but rather by his emphasis on the essentially authorial techniques of dialogue and character formation which permit the poles of consciousness to interact while maintaining their fundamental difference from each other" (80). The basis of these authorial techniques is, of course, language. Central to the formation of the self, therefore, is the language of the self, a concern that occupies another major thinker in our century: Jacques Lacan. Let us, then, see what a comparison or combination of Bakhtin and Lacan can reveal about the connections between authorship and the creation of the self.

THREE

Bakhtin and Lacan

Author, Hero, and
the Language of the Self

By now the influence of Mikhail Bakhtin and Jacques Lacan on literary studies is well established, particularly with respect to our notion of literature and our interaction with literary texts. Unlike many theorists, however, Bakhtin not only develops a concept of literature but also examines the creation of literature—what he calls "the aesthetic event"—and its parallel to interhuman relationships. Todorov says in his book on Bakhtin: "Artistic creation cannot be analyzed apart from a theory of alterity" (166); that is, artistic creation always entails interaction between an I and an other. Clark and Holquist explain, "That which in his [Bakhtin's] epistemology is modeled as the I/other distinction becomes in his aesthetics the distinction between the author, who occupies a position analogous to the self, and the hero, who occupies a position analogous to the other. This movement is rehearsed each time the text is read, as the reader becomes the flesh of the author's meaning, a self transgradient to the text's otherness" (87-88).

Bakhtin explores the implications of this approach in "Author and Hero in Aesthetic Activity," where he pursues the relation between writer and character and the impact of that relation on the life of the self. Here, as everywhere, Bakhtin's touchstone is discourse, or the word. The author, he tells us, "must become *other* to himself, must look upon himself through the eyes of another" (*Estetika* 8), and this is accomplished through the word. Indeed, the scene of any text or utterance has aesthetic and existential ramifications for the self. Clark and Holquist observe, "The sce-

nario of any utterance must contain the same three *dramatis person-
ae:* the speaker, the listener, and the topic. All utterances are born,
live, and die in the drama that is played out in the interaction
between these participants. In order to emphasize the drama-
turgical aspects of these forces, Bakhtin anthropomorphizes the
topic, since it is the one element of the triad that might otherwise
appear to be a nonhuman actor. He calls it 'the hero' of the playet
which unfolds in any utterance" (205). In creating a hero, the
author also anthropomorphizes a topic or an idea. The author thus
stands in a relation to his text similar to the self's relation to
consciousness as shaped by discourse. What Heidegger says of the
relation between the artist and his work is true: "The artist is the
origin of the work. The work is the origin of the artist" (*Poetry* 17).
And the same statement may be made about the relation of the
author to his hero. For the hero is the constitutive feature of the
author's work.

Like Bakhtin, Lacan approaches the self in terms of a discourse
between the self and its other, but from a psychoanalytic standpoint, concerned particularly with that discourse as it unfolds
between analyst and patient. Shoshana Felman, commenting on
the connection between this relation and how we view a literary
text, has noted, "The text has for us authority—the very type of
authority by which Jacques Lacan indeed defines the role of the
psychoanalyst in the structure of transference. Like the analyst
viewed by the patient, the text is viewed by us as 'a subject
presumed to know'—as the very place where meaning, and *knowledge* of meaning, reside" ("Open" 7). What concerns us here,
however, is not so much how we regard the text as what happens in
the creation of the text.

Lacan pursues this issue most extensively in "The Function of
Language in Psychoanalysis" (in *The Language of the Self*), where he
connects the structure of the self with the structure of language
and explains the implications of that structure for psychoanalysis.
In the opening pages of that work, for example, Lacan describes
the position of the analyst by saying,

> If the first thing to make itself heard is the void, it is within
> himself that he will experience it, and it is beyond the Word
> that he will seek a reality to fill this void. . . . But what in fact

was this appeal from the subject beyond the void of his speech? It was an appeal to Truth in its ultimate nature, through which other appeals resulting from humbler needs will find faltering expression. But first and foremost it was the appeal of the void, in the ambiguous *béance* of an attempted seduction of the other by the means on which the subject has come completely to rely and to which he is going to commit the monumental construct of his narcissism. [9]

Already we have the hint of a parallel between a verbal construct and a text in which the truth of the self is worked out. Of special interest to the concern at hand, then, is the matter of what light Lacan's insights on the language of the self may shed on Bakhtin's understanding of the author/hero relation.

A comparison of Bakhtin and Lacan will show that the author's relation to his hero is a relation of the self to itself mediated by the other. As Todorov has explained it, Bakhtin distinguishes two stages in every act of the author: one is identification, and the other is "an inverse movement, whereby the novelist re-integrates his own position. For this second act of creative endeavor, Bakhtin uses the neologism *vnenakhodimost'* or 'finding oneself outside' " (153). As the author's other, the hero is the middle term through which the author reintegrates and thus authors himself: the I comes to itself by way of the other. What Bakhtin says of "the idea" in *Problems of Dostoevsky's Poetics* is also true of the self: "The idea is a *live* event, played out at the point of dialogic meeting between two or several consciousnesses. In this sense the idea is similar to the *word,* with which it is dialogically united" (88). If, as Bakhtin claims, "the novel always includes in itself the activity of coming to know another's word" (*Dialogic* 353), that activity—the aesthetic event—is the process by which the author approaches himself as a living subject by way of his relation to the fictional hero. Felman reminds us in this regard that "the analytical experience, says Lacan, has been involved, since its very origins, not simply with fiction, but with the 'truthful' structural necessity of fiction, that is, with its symbolic non-arbitrariness" ("Beyond" 1044). Like the truth of the word or the truth of the idea, the truth of the self emerges through encounter, and encounter has the structure of fiction. Thus we hear Bakhtin declare, "In the aesthetic event we have an encounter between two consciousnesses . . . , where the consciousness of the author stands in a relation to the consciousness of the hero—not from the standpoint of his [the hero's] thematic composition or thematically objective significance but from the standpoint of his living subjective unity" (*Estetika* 79-80). When consciousness encounters consciousness, word encounters word. "No signification can be sustained," Lacan writes, "other than by reference to another signification" (*Écrits* 150)—by reference to another word or consciousness: meaning turns on encounter.

In the dialogical meeting between author and hero, the self encounters itself through its response to the other, a response in which the "author speaks not *about* a character, but *with* him" (Bakhtin, *Problems* 63). "Every word calls for a reply," Lacan insists (*Language* 9), echoing Bakhtin's view that "the speaker himself is situated in an actively responsive understanding; he awaits not a passive understanding . . . but a reply" (*Estetika* 247). The character speaks, and the author listens, so that he may reply to the character and to himself. Two main points to be addressed in this essay, then, are the movement of the author as I and the role of the hero as other.

As we shall see, however, there is one more dimension of the relation that must be considered if we are to address the truth of the relation, and this is where a comparison of Bakhtin and Lacan will perhaps prove most helpful. This third aspect is precisely the Third, what Lacan terms *the Other*, who stands in a third position, apart from the author and his hero, apart from the I and the other. In *Freudianism*, Voloshinov offers one description of this arrangement by saying, "*Any locution said aloud or written down for intelligible communication* (i.e., anything but words merely reposing in a dictionary) *is the expression and product of the social interaction of three participants: the speaker* (author), *the listener* (reader), *and the topic* (the who or what) *of speech* (the hero)" (105). Putting Voloshinov's statement into the context at hand, we here regard the author as I, the hero as other, and the implied reader (the Third) as the Other, the witness and judge of the interaction between author and hero. For Bakhtin and Lacan (although they have their differences, as we shall see), the Other represents the realm of truth; it is through the presence of the Other that truth can be a question in the author's effort to create his work of art and that there can be any issues surrounding a language of the self. Constituted by the word, the self thus entails not only a relation to the other but also a relation to a third.

It will be noted too that the Other situates truth beyond the reality it concerns, beyond data. We assume that the author struggles to address the truth of a certain reality; through his work he engages in "an uninterrupted mutual interaction with the discourse of life," as Bakhtin puts it (*Dialogic* 383), and the discourse of life always includes more than the reality at hand. For an overwhelming part of that discourse concerns what ought to be and what is yet to be. We shall discover further that since truth is in a third position beyond a given reality, it is only through the literary discourse or the fictional structure that the author can deal with the truth of the world, of his hero, and of himself. As Lacan has observed, "it is from somewhere other than the Reality it concerns that Truth derives its guarantee: it is from Speech [the Word]. Just as it is from Speech that Truth receives the mark that establishes it in a fictional structure" (*Écrits* 305-6). One will recall in this connection Foucault's remark that "language always seems to be inhabited by the other, the elsewhere, the distant; it is hollowed by absence. Is it not the locus in which something other than itself appears, does not its own existence seem to be dissipated in this function?" (*Archaeology* 111). Only the fictional structure—the hero called forth by the author's word—can take the human being "elsewhere," to the place from which truth is derived. Indeed, truth, like the self, is always somewhere else, always fictional.

The fictional structure of truth does not lie in artifice or falsehood but in the open-endedness of truth as what is *not yet*, unfinalized and forever in question. Like the character himself, it is in a continual state of development, unfolding and living in a process of hearing and responding. As something yet to be fulfilled, truth is thus dialogical. Or perhaps better: truth lies in the dialogical quest for truth, a quest that, Bakhtin argues, characterizes discourse in the novel (*Problems* 110). In creating the novel, the author enters into a dialogue with his hero for the sake of truth, which is in a third position—for the sake of the Other, who is the witness and judge of the aesthetic endeavor. Aesthetics thus becomes not only a matter concerning form but an issue involving the very life of the I who engages the other in the presence of the Other. That life is grounded in the word as the language of the self; again, the author who creates a hero in his literary text also creates the text of himself: the self is a literary locus. Let us proceed, then, with the help of Bakhtin and Lacan, to an analysis of this interrelation and an argument for this thesis.

THE MOVEMENT OF THE AUTHOR AS I

While the author of a literary text may not create his work out of nothing, the first thing to make itself heard, the first thing to cry out from the blank page, is the void within himself, as well as the void within which he becomes a self. This "within" is not a secret place tucked away inside the body but the "reverting," to use Levinas's words, that "concerns me and circumscribes me and orders me by my own voice" (*Otherwise* 197). In the case at hand, it is the "within" of the author's relationship with his character when that character is as yet without body, when his word has yet to become flesh. "Experiencing the spatiality of a person's external boundaries," Bakhtin has noted, "is a special and extremely important moment in the external, plastic-pictorial vision of him," explaining that it is "the moment of man's limitation in the world. In self-consciousness, this outward boundary is experienced quite differently, that is, in the self's relation to itself, as compared to the relation to another person. Indeed, only in another person is a living, aesthetic (and ethical), convincing experience of human finitude given to me" (*Estetika* 34).

In the authorial context, the self-consciousness Bakhtin invokes is what the author must move into by establishing a moment of limitation—a body—that distinguishes his hero. Until he can embrace his hero, "in all the moments of his being, his body, and *in it* his soul" (Bakhtin, *Estetika* 39), the author himself is yet to be. The author as I, then, is confronted with the "recurrence to oneself" Levinas describes when he says, "This recurrence is incarnation. In it the body which makes giving possible makes one *other* without alienating. For this other is the heart, and the goodness of the same, the inspiration or the very psyche in the soul" (*Otherwise* 109). And so the author is inspired—as the one who is yet to be. It is the absence of self that launches the author into a movement toward himself. His presence in the text arises from an absence before the page. In the words of Lacan, "being of non-being, that is how *I* as subject comes on the scene" (*Écrits* 300). From this zero point the author must move toward a point of difference or noncoincidence with himself, where the I struggles to speak a language of the self and with the self.

"The genuine life of the personality," Bakhtin has observed, "takes place at the point of non-coincidence between a man and himself. . . . The genuine life of the personality is made available only through a *dialogic* penetration of that personality" (*Problems* 59). In the case of the author, the point of noncoincidence with himself lies at the point of his pen, as it were; it is the point where he is about to speak but has not yet spoken, where he is about to say in the language of another—of his hero—"here I am." This point of noncoincidence is rather like the Valley of Decision, where, in deciding something about the other, the author decides something about himself. The movement of the author as I is made of decisiveness. His dialogical penetration of himself occurs in a penetration of the hero as other, whom he addresses and by whom he is addressed. Here the author approaches the point of noncoincidence with himself by becoming coincident with the hero. Discussing this movement, Bakhtin writes, "I must experience—must see and discover—what he experiences; I must take up his position as though I were coincident with him" (*Estetika* 24-25). This "taking up a position" is what sets the author into the movement of dialogical relation, a movement propelled by the word. The hero asks, "What have you made of me?" and the author's response is the making of himself. For in the word he finds the resonance of other voices that make it possible for him to become other to himself and thereby create his character as well as himself. It is true in a double sense that, in Bakhtin's words, "the novel always includes in itself the activity of coming to know another's word" (*Dialogic* 353)—true not only of the character-to-character relation but of the author-to-character relation. This "coming to know" lies in the "taking up a position," which is the movement of the author as an I.

For the author, "subjectivity is the other in the same," to borrow a phrase from Levinas (*Otherwise* 25). In order to be tangible to

himself, the author must make his hero tangible, must, again, give
the hero a body that the author can touch and thus be touched by.
This he achieves by placing the word in the mouth of the hero like a
creator breathing a soul into his character. And the breath he
breathes is the breath he draws: dialogically generating a presence
in relation to his hero, the author is summoned as he summons.
The question his hero puts to him is the question he must put to
himself: What are you making of me? This splitting of the self in
the address to itself is a wounding of the self whereby the hero
emerges from the author as from a wound transformed into a
womb. To create is to be wounded: inscription entails infliction, so
that the movement of the author as I is a movement out of a
wound. The tangibility of the hero arises from the vulnerability of
the author. Tangibility and vulnerability, then, are constituent
features of the author's dialogical relation to his hero, as well as to
himself. Inasmuch as the author's relation to the hero is dialogical,
moreover, his responsibility for the hero is of a piece with his
response to the hero; he is both accountable for and accountable to
the other. If he endeavors to create a hero whom he can recognize
(in every sense of the word), he also seeks recognition from the
hero, for it is by way of the hero's recognition that he recognizes
himself. Lacan has pointed out that "the first object of desire" on
the part of the I "is to be recognized by the other" (*Language* 31),
since this is the basis of self-recognition.

Hence the author's subjectivity is grounded in the discourse
through which he moves into his hero by his hero's movement out
of him. Says Lacan, "The form alone in which Language is expressed defines subjectivity. Language says: 'you will go such and
such a way, and when you see such and such, you will turn off in
such and such a direction.' In other words, it refers itself to the
discourse of the other. As such, it is enveloped in the highest
function of the Word, inasmuch as the Word commits its author by
investing the person to whom it is addressed with a new reality"
(*Language* 61-62). Lacan's accent on the form of language reminds
us of Bakhtin's insistence that "*form is a limit* aesthetically treated.
The point here concerns a limit of the body, a limit of the soul, a
limit of the spirit" (*Estetika* 81). Later he asserts, "from a meth-
odological standpoint, the problem of the soul is an aesthetic
problem" (*Estetika* 89). The formal difficulties that characterize

the aesthetics of the self, however, rest not only on what lies within the limits of the self but on what lies beyond those limits. The language that says, "You will go," is *other* to the self; because that language is other, the author can create a hero who is other. What is the "highest function of the Word"? To create, to make new. The reality of the self lies in the new reality with which it invests the other. Thus the very life of the self, the genuine personality, is at stake in the author's becoming as though coincident with his hero.

Orienting himself toward the discourse of the other, the author questions his hero by questioning himself. "The artist's struggle for a stable, well-defined image of the hero," Bakhtin argues, "is largely a struggle with himself" (*Estetika* 8). This struggle or inquiry is not only a process of creating the hero but also a process of bearing witness, a reckoning before the other. Creation is response and is therefore couched in responsibility. Here too Lacan can help. "What I seek in the Word," he tells us, "is the response of the other. What constitutes me as subject is my question. In order to be recognized by the other, I utter what was in view of what will be. In order to find him, I call him by a name which he must assume or refuse in order to reply to me" (*Language* 63). What the author seeks in the word is the voice of his hero, who is created out of the questions that make the author who he is. Writing his text according to what has been, he places his hero in the past with a view toward what, he, the hero, will be: the author moves forward in the past tense. In this way the author becomes I through the discourse of the other by which his hero is invested with a reality constituted by the word. In that word and its reality lies the response of the hero. It is out of that reality of his own, out of a word of his own, that the hero takes on the name that makes him other, one who can reply to his author.

An observation from Heidegger's essay "Language" may help here: "This naming does not hand out titles, does not apply terms, but calls into the word. The naming calls. Calling brings closer what it calls" (*Poetry* 198). The hero's reply to the calling is, again, a question that resonates in the name conferred upon him. If the names of Quixote, Hamlet, Faust, and Raskolnikov call us out, so too must they have questioned their authors, calling them out from the security of holding a position. Dialogue is movement into the open, leaving behind all protection, every guarantee. Once more we realize that dialogue is vulnerability. As the author listens and responds to the hero, he moves along the track of the hero's movement, coming into being and disappearing from the hero's discourse: he speaks without hearing himself speak. The danger, as Lacan expresses it, is that "I identify myself in Language, but only by losing myself in it like an object" (*Language* 63). No sooner does the author situate himself and his hero than the flow of discourse takes both of them elsewhere: the author is a locus dissipated by the other—by his hero—and by language itself.

The movement, however, does not end in a loss or disappearance, as Lacan's assertion in "The Subversion of the Subject" suggests: "There where it was just now, there where it was for a while, between an extinction that is still glowing and a birth that is retarded, 'I' can come into being and disappear from what I say. . . . The relation of the subject to the signifier . . . is embodied in an enunciation (*énonciation*) whose being trembles with the vascillation that comes back to it from its own statement (*enoncé*)" (*Écrits* 300). With this we discern more clearly what happens to the author in his utterance of what has been in the past tense of his narrative. The extinction Lacan refers to is the *was* by which the author gives voice to his character; the retarded birth pertains to what the author is yet to be by virtue of his relation to the hero. And so we may better understand Bakhtin's remark in "Author and Hero" that "for me, memory is memory of the future; for the other, it is memory of the past" (*Estetika* 110).

This diachrony of time is also a diachrony of identity, as Levinas has shown: "It is as a senescence beyond the recuperation of memory that time, lost time that does not return, is a diachrony, and concerns me. This diachrony of time is not due to the length of the interval. . . . It is a disjunction of identity where the same does not rejoin the same" (*Otherwise* 52). The problem that confronts the self cannot be resolved by changing tenses or persons in the narrative itself; it is not a question of content but of creating through a process of saying. Language itself, as a structure of the self, determines the disappearance of the saying of the I into the said. This disappearance is a result of the fact that, in Voloshinov's words, "the object of self-observation is the inner sign, which, as such, can also be an outer sign" (*Marksizm* 40). But since saying occurs in the light of the said, the author may return as I out of the said, moving, as it were, from the inner sign to the outer sign and back. The author as I may be heard through his hero as an echo, but only as an echo, only as a trace. For the dialogical relation is never finalized, forever unsettled. Its openness lies in its open-endedness. The I is born only to die and be born again by dialogically penetrating the symbols of the said in a new movement of saying. We understand, then, the seriousness of the risk Gide speaks of when he says, "The literary creator who seeks himself runs a great risk—the risk of finding himself. From then onwards he writes coldly, deliberately, in keeping with the self he has found. He imitates himself. . . . His great dread is no longer insincerity, but inconsistency" (50). In this imitation, in this dread, in this "finding" of oneself, saying comes to a halt.

The occasion for the penetration of the symbol and the movement of saying is the hero's gift to the author, and it enables the author to realize a being-for-death. There is no creation except among the shadows of death; the author emerges as I by rolling away the stone of the said that sealed him in the tomb of the symbol. As the gift is given, however, the Great Debt is incurred. "Thus it is the virtue of the *verbe*," Lacan declares, "which perpetuates the movement of the Great Debt" *(Language* 41). And, he goes on to say, "Symbols in fact envelop the life of a man in a network so total that . . . they give the words which will make him faithful or renegade, the law of the acts which will follow him right to the very place where he *is* not yet and beyond his death itself; and so total that through them his end finds its meaning in the last judgment where the *verbe* absolves his being or condemns it—except he attain the subjective bringing to realization of being-for-death" (42). Only the one to whom we are in debt can absolve or condemn us, and the author's debt is to the word. For through the word the author is able to penetrate the symbol in a dialogical encounter with the symbol. Here, in Bakhtin's words, "languages are dialogically implicated *in* each other and begin to exist *for* each other" *(Dialogic* 400). In his "bringing to realization" a "being-for-death" through a process of perpetual dying and rebirth—in the act of creation—the author implicates the symbol that had implicated and thus enveloped him.

This reversal, this movement forward in a turning back, is what distinguishes the hero as character from the hero as type.

"Character is in the past," Bakhtin writes, "type in the present. . . . A type is a necessary feature of some kind of environment" (*Estetika* 159-60). A type, in Lacan's terms, is the product of an inventory of symbols. Moving toward the other side of the symbol to make his hero a character, the author approaches the trace of his I, where the echo of the Word (*parole*) abides in the word (*verbe*) and is heard in his being-for-death. His mortality is the origin of his meaning, and his meaning the origin of his immortality. We can see, therefore, that what Lacan says of the relation between the I and the other applies to the relation between author and hero: "If he identifies himself with the other, it is by fixing him solidly in the metamorphosis of his essential image, and no being is ever evoked by him except among the shadows of death" (*Language* 85). The author's hero is the death of him. Hence he lives.

Early on we cited Bakhtin's statement that the author must become as though coincident with the hero; in order to live as I, the author must become other to himself. From what has been said, we discover that this movement finds its highest expression in a being-for-death that is a dying for the sake of the other. We are reminded in this regard of Clark and Holquist's observation that Dostoevsky was something of a Christ to his heroes (249) and of Bakhtin's statement on the Christ in "Author and Hero": "In Christ we find, in all its depth, the single synthesis of *ethical solipsism,* of infinite severity of man toward himself—that is, an irreproachably pure relation to himself—with *ethical-aesthetic goodness* toward the other: here for the first time appears an infinitely profound *I-for-myself,* . . . immeasurably good to the other, rendering the whole truth to the other as such, revealing and confirming in all its fullness the precious originality of the other. . . . Christ opposes *I* and the *other:* absolute sacrifice for himself, absolute charity for the other" (*Estetika* 51-52). In order to become coincident with the other, the self must die away from itself; the author must not survive his hero, and yet he survives. It is his status as a survivor, then, that constitutes the author's Great Debt. The self is the one accused, the one who is in the accusative without a nominative. There was once a Hasidic master who made his farewells to his family each time he went off to pray, certain that he would die in the saying of his prayers. So it must be for the author in the saying of his literary work, in the dialogue with his hero. For the literary endeavor has much in common with prayer. Like prayer, it draws the word from language in an offering to the Other, the word in which the Other is manifested. The Other here is both subject and object, just as the author is both I and other.

It is no accident that the theme of the double has come to be so prevalent in literature and that within that theme we find the threat of death surrounding the identity of the I in relation to the other. For this theme, which concerns the literary character, also reflects the relation of the author to his hero. It will be helpful to recall an insight from Foucault on this point: "Is death not that upon the basis of which knowledge in general is possible—so much so that we can think of it as being, in the area of psychoanalysis, the figure of that empirico-transcendental *duplication* that characterizes man's mode of being within finitude?" (*Order* 375). It is the death of the author *for* the hero that makes him the author *of* the hero. Death distinguishes the author as the I who has disappeared into the text where the other finds his place; it lays claim to the author and makes him into an I torn from the They. Hence in death, to use Heidegger's phrase, "it is revealed to Dasein that in this distinctive possibility for itself, it breaks away from *das Man*" (*Sein* 263). And it is his being-for-death that enables the author to tear the creative word from the idle talk of the crowd. The movement of the author as I is a movement toward death. When it is for the other, death marks the deliverance of the imprisoned sense and is the liberation and revelation of the I, of the language of the self. It is the thing that wins for the self the pardon of the word.

And so we may better understand Lacan when he says, "Hieroglyphics of hysteria, blazons of phobia, labyrinths of the *Zwangsneurose*—charms of impotence, enigmas of inhibition, oracles of anxiety—talking arms of character, seals of self-punishment, disguises of perversion—these are the hermetic elements that our exegesis resolves, the equivocations that our invocation dissolves, the artifices that our dialect absolves, in a deliverance of the imprisoned sense, which moves from the revelation of the palimpsest to the given word of the mystery and to the pardon of the Word" (*Language* 44). The "deliverance of the imprisoned sense" in this case is the deliverance of the hero from the author as a child might be delivered from the womb—or a man from the tomb. The hero is the word within the author's word, the text beneath the text, which is revealed—like "the revelation of the palimpsest"— as the author becomes other, coincident with his hero. The blazons of phobia, oracles of anxiety, and so on constitute the monological discourse of the I-for-myself that the author must dissolve or transform into the dialogical discourse of the I-for-the-other. The consciousness, and therefore the language, of the self is constantly played off against the other's consciousness, making the language of the self other to itself. Thus the word of the other is the breath by which the self lives. Let us consider now the role of the hero in this capacity as the other who brings deliverance and absolution to the author.

THE ROLE OF THE HERO AS OTHER

Bakhtin's definition of character in "Author and Hero" is a good place to begin this inquiry. "By *character*," he writes, "we mean that form of interrelation between hero and author which carries out the task of creating a whole hero as a defined personality" (*Estetika* 151). In this statement we notice first of all that the character is an *event* or a movement by which the hero comes into being, and not a static category or type. We also notice once more, and with added significance, that the character is rather like the idea Bakhtin speaks of when he says, "The idea is a *live event*, played out at the point of dialogic meeting between two or several consciousnesses" (*Problems* 88). Dostoevsky, for example, does not precisely make ideas into characters, as Berdyaev has claimed (*Dostoevsky* 35); he creates heroes out of ideas. If the character gives rise to the hero from a position between author and hero, however, then the author's relation to the hero is a relation to a personality who is *not yet*, who is forever yet to emerge from character as a complete personality. What Bakhtin says of the human being also applies to the hero as a "defined" personality: "A man never coincides with himself. One cannot apply to him the formula A = A. . . . The genuine life of the personality takes place at the point of non-coincidence between a man and himself" (*Problems* 59). Since the subjectivity of the author is rooted in the hero—the same in the other—the author, too, is one who is *not yet*. If character, in this sense, carries out the task of creating a hero, it also serves to define the author as the one who stands in a relation to the hero as other. It is by virtue of a concept of character as an idea, as a live event, that the hero thus confronts the author with a meaningful future, with the project of becoming a self in the process of creating the literary hero.

This last point should be kept in mind when we hear Bakhtin say, "In itself, the definition given to me lies not in the categories of temporal being but in the categories of the *not-yet-existing*, in the categories of purpose and meaning, in the meaningful future, which is at odds with anything I have at hand in the past or present. To be myself for myself means yet becoming myself (*to cease becoming myself . . . means spiritual death*)" (*Estetika* 109). What Anthony Wilden notes as a similarity between Heidegger and Lacan, then, is also a similarity to Bakhtin: "With Heidegger, Lacan views the subject as subordinated to language and thus cuts across the distinction often made between interpersonal and intrapersonal relations by representing the second as a subset of the first in the chain of signifiers which link them" (200). The intrapersonal relation by which I become myself turns on the interpersonal relation to the other. "Only because Dasein is defined by selfhood," Heidegger states it, "can an I-self relate 'itself' to a Thou-self. Selfhood is the presupposition of the possibility of being an 'I,' which itself is revealed only in the Thou" (*Essence* 87). In itself, the definition given to the author originates from the hero as other, or rather from the author's dialogical relation to the hero as other. Because that relation is dialogical, it is unfinalized, lying in the categories of the not-yet-existing; the role of the hero, then, is to place the author in those categories, which constitute purpose and meaning. As a personality, the hero is in process and thereby implicates the author as one who is in process, turned over to the meaningful future.

If the author as I, moreover, is at odds with anything at hand, then the hero as other is at odds with anything on the page. He too belongs to a process of becoming himself, and the author's ability to launch the hero into such a process turns on his own activity of becoming. The hero emerges, therefore, from the literary discourse that engages the author in a language of the self, a language of becoming, which is a literary language, in contrast to the idle talk of everyday chitchat, scientific analysis, or journalistic reporting. In his capacity as other, the hero plays an essential role in the life of the author, making it an interactive life characterized by a process of becoming. The role of the hero, in short, is to bring the author to life.

Thus a major role of the hero as other is, in the words of Bakhtin, to announce that "the *other* is first of all *I-for-myself*" (*Estetika* 52). Making the author other to himself, the hero enables the author to discover the other in the same, to realize that what is for the other is for the self. Not only must the author create his hero, but he must care for him as a parent might care for a child; he must care with a caring that is a form of responsibility. Here I-for-myself becomes I-who-am-responsible; as the other, the hero makes the author into such an I. If, as Bakhtin argues, "the life of the word is contained in its transfer from one mouth to another" (*Problems* 202), so too is the life of the self contained in its offering to the other. Indeed, the transfer of the word is the offering of the self; Bakhtin expresses it in "Author and Hero" by saying, "The soul is the gift of my spirit to the other" (*Estetika* 116). In the case of the author, word is transformed into spirit in the transfer of the author's word from his mouth to the mouth of his hero. If he is to create a language of and for the self, then the author is there for the hero, not the other way around. His task is to transfer his word to his hero, the lifeblood of his voice into the hero's voice, and thereby to bring life to the word—and to the self—in a living language of the self. In his role as other the hero thus posits the author's *there*, by way of which he arrives at his *here* in a transfer from himself to himself: the other is first of all I-for-myself.

What Bakhtin says of the hero in *Problems of Dostoevsky's Poetics* is true: "His consciousness of self is constantly perceived against the background of the other's consciousness of him—'I for myself' against the background of 'I for another.' Thus the hero's words about himself are structured under the continuous influence of someone else's words about him" (207). This is the "profound and unresolved conflict with another's word" Bakhtin mentions in "Discourse in the Novel" (*Dialogic* 346). And because it is a conflict with the word, it is a conflict with the self, so that the same statement can be made about the author's relation to the hero: we must bear in mind that the "someone else" here includes the author and that the hero's I-for-myself resonates as the author's I-for-the-other. Indeed, Bakhtin himself reminds us of this: "The author's design for a character is a *design for discourse*. Thus the author's discourse about a character is discourse about discourse. It is oriented toward the hero as if toward a discourse, and is therefore dialogically *addressed* to him. By the very construction of the novel, the author speaks not *about* a character but *with* him. And it cannot be otherwise: only a dialogic and participating orientation takes another person's discourse seriously" (*Problems* 63-64). The author's subject, in other words, is the language of the self; this is an important ramification of Bakhtin's claim that "in the novel, literary language possesses an organ for perceiving the heterodox nature of its own speech. Heteroglossia-in-itself becomes, in the novel and thanks to the novel, heteroglossia-for-itself: languages are dialogically implicated *in* each other and begin to exist *for* each other" (*Dialogic* 400). The author listens as he speaks, responds as he summons; speaking with the hero, he is addressed in his address to the hero.

So it is equally important to note that the author's word about himself is uttered against the background—or through the foreground—of the hero's word. If the author says "I am I" in someone else's language, he also says "I am other" in his own. Bakhtin makes this point in *The Dialogic Imagination* (315), and Lacan expresses it by declaring, "What this structure of the signifying chain discloses is the possibility I have, precisely in so far as I have this language in common with other subjects, that is to say, in so far as it exists as a language, to use it in order to signify *something quite other* than what it says" (*Écrits* 155). This is the saying, the process of coming to know another's word, that makes a language of the self possible. And, as Bakhtin suggests, it is also a definitive feature of the novel: "The novel always includes in itself the activity of coming to know another's word, a coming to knowledge whose process is represented in the novel" (*Dialogic* 353). To have a self is to have the capacity to speak as another self, and the hero fosters this capacity in the author. This is, in part, what the novel is about.

In addition to providing him with a capacity, the hero puts to the author a question concerning the substance or soul of the author himself. Once again, Bakhtin's claim concerning the hero in Dostoevsky's works underscores not only the hero's position within the novel but his relation to the author as well: "The hero interests Dostoevsky as a *particular point of view on the world and on oneself,* as the position enabling a person to interpret and evaluate his own self and his surrounding reality" (*Problems* 47). The world is constituted by discourse and the self by its place in that discourse. When author encounters hero, discourse encounters discourse, world confronts world, self collides with self. The role of the hero? To provide the author with a point of collision with himself. The hero's "I am I" entails both an evaluation of his own self and a self-evaluation or self-penetration on the part of the author. "The way in which I create myself is by means of a quest," we read in Clark and Holquist. "I go out to the other in order to come back with a self" (78). In his capacity as other the hero brings the author to self-consciousness in the dialogical process of creating the hero. Dialogue with the other is dialogue with the self, not before the mirror as Lacan might conceive it but on the threshold, at a turning point in the life of the soul. In contrast to Lacan, Bakhtin views the mirror not as a point of stasis but as part of the movement in the life of the self. Clark and Holquist, in fact, have noted this point of opposition between Bakhtin and Lacan, explaining that "when I complete the other, or when the other completes me, she and I are actually exchanging the gift of a perceptible self. This is what Bakthin means when he argues that we get our selves from others. . . . As opposed to Lacan, Bakhtin conceives the mirror stage as coterminous with consciousness; it is endless as long as we are in the process of creating ourselves" (79). For the author, there is no question of release from the mirror of the hero. The task, rather, is to sustain his interaction with the hero.

Although, as indicated, there are important differences between Lacan's notion of the mirror stage and Bakhtin's concept of self-consciousness, Wilden makes a statement that suggests some similarities. "Lacan," he tells us, "regards the *stade du miroir*—the vision of harmony by a being in discord—as at the origin of the phantasy of the *corps morcelé* " (174). The author, indeed, is a being in discord. The *corps morcelé,* or the fragmented body, however, is no dream; it is a distinguishing feature of the reality of creation. In the interaction with the hero, the self tears away from itself, rends itself, so that the hero issues from the wound he inflicts and then penetrates that wound to draw forth the author turned inside out,

as it were. His interior is thus externalized, and the author approaches what Bakhtin calls the *inner man*, " 'one's own self,'
accessible not to passive self-observation but only through an *active
dialogic approach to one's own self*, destroying the naive wholeness of
one's notions about the self" (*Problems* 120). The author does not
observe himself by staring at the hero; he listens to himself by
speaking through the hero. The dialogical interchange between
author and hero is a movement inward through a movement
outward, into the open, to a position of vulnerability, where the
between gapes like a wound. The "inner man" is the man between
himself and the other, exposed through his interaction with the
other. The author speaks and breaks. And the hero—the one who
emerges as a question in the utterance—is the one upon whom is
broken the "naive wholeness" of the author's notions about himself.

As the author is undone or unsettled, however, so is the hero. He
who poses a question becomes a question and is thereby thrown
into the categories of purpose and meaning, into the *not yet*, which
is the place where the hero begins to take on a soul. If I stand on
the threshold in my approach to the other, so too is the other on the
threshold. It is the other, in fact, who defines the relation as a
threshold. Hence we have Bakhtin's observation that "Dostoevsky
always represents a person on the *threshold* of a final decision, at a
moment of *crisis*, at an unfinalizable—and *unpredeterminable*—turning point for the soul" (*Problems* 61). In "Discourse in the Novel"
Bakhtin writes, "Discourse lives, as it were, on the boundary
between its own context and another, alien context. . . . Dialogic
inter-orientation becomes, as it were, an event of discourse itself"
(*Dialogic* 284). As ever, what is said here of discourse also applies to
the human being. At the threshold the human being takes on
substance through decisiveness, since no predetermined word, no
ready-made reply, can take the place of his voice. What is required
is the man himself; what is required is response. The person is,
again, on the threshold because "his consciousness of self is constantly perceived against the background of the other's consciousness of him" (Bakhtin, *Problems* 207). From the standpoint of
the author, then, the hero is not only on the threshold—he *is* the
threshold, the turning point for the soul, where the author is made
of his responsibility. At the turning point for the soul, the author's

self-consciousness is born in the self's turning in on itself: as the
other turns inward, so does the I. Inwardness requires the *between*
comprising both I and other.

In this connection Bakhtin notes, "Self-consciousness, as the
artistic dominant governing the construction of a character, cannot
lie alongside other features of his image; it absorbs these other
features into itself as its own material and deprives them of any
power to define and finalize the hero" (*Problems* 50). Self-consciousness is the breeder of crisis, and the crisis is the stuff out of
which the character is constructed. Since crisis is what is yet to be
resolved, it is the material of the character himself, and not an
accident that befalls him. Self-consciousness, therefore, is not a
feature of his image—it *is* his image. If self-consciousness is the
artistic dominant governing the construction of the hero, then the
self-consciousness of the hero is also that of the author. In dialogic
relation I come before the other as a self before another self in such
a way that consciousness of self is of a piece with consciousness of
the other, each endlessly acting on the other. Thus, within the
dialogical relation, both author and hero are unfinalized. Coming
to the threshold of the open, each enters into open-endedness.
There, in the open air of open-endedness, the author breathes the
life of self-consciousness into the hero, and the hero into the
author. And the living breath of both is the dialogical word, or the
word of the other, which is always the subject of the novel, always
its hero. The novel deals with life because it deals with the word.
The novel is made of the force of life.

Death, on the other hand, comes by finalization, enclosure. If
the hero is endangered by death, the threat to him comes from
those features of his image—from the symbols—that might suffo-
cate and seal him into a fixed form, where he would be no longer
the other but an *it*. This threat of the symbol, however, constitutes
the urgency and the endlessness of the author's endeavor. At this
point it may help to invoke Lacan: "Thus the symbol manifests
itself first of all as the murderer of the thing, and this death constitutes in the subject the eternalization of his desire. The first
symbol in which we recognize humanity in its vestigial traces is the
sepulture, and the intermediary of death can be recognized in
every relation where man comes to the life of his history" (*Language*

84). Enclosed in his desire, as in a sepulture, the subject's first longing is for the relation to the other who may bring him to life. In that longing he turns to the symbols that signal and sanction the relation, seeking the signs of recognition from the other. No sooner does he have the symbol, however, than the symbol eclipses the relation and seals the subject in the tomb of the sign. The subject in the case before us is the author, and the thing he desires is a living hero, a hero who is a self in response to whom the author can voice a language of the self. But as soon as the symbol situates the hero, it occludes him; the body of the symbol gets in the way of his breath and blood. The author's task, then, is to create and then penetrate those signs by which a hero can be recognized, to move to the other side of the word already uttered, which, in the words of Bakhtin, is "the dead flesh of meaning" (*Estetika* 117). Placing his hero within the tomb of the said, in the dead letter of the symbol, the author must constantly roll away the stone that inters his hero—and himself—through the saying of an unending dialogue.

Bakhtin describes the desired outcome of this interaction in "Author and Hero" by saying, "The life of the hero begins to strive to break through the form and rhythm, to obtain an authoritative, meaningful significance. . . . An artistically convincing completion becomes impossible: the soul of the hero shifts from the category of *other* to the category of *I*—it disperses and loses itself in spirit" (*Estetika* 116). The hero, in other words, strives to become free, where "freedom," as Berdyaev expresses it, "sets itself up against the exclusive domination of the formal element and the building of barriers" (*Dostoevsky* 73-74). The formal or symbolic element is the element of the settled and the static. It has a grounding function, as Lacan suggests when he says, "The Symbolic function presents itself as a double movement within the subject: man makes an object of his action, but only in order to restore to this action in due time its place as a grounding" (*Language* 48). Shifting from other to I, the hero moves into the open dynamics of the unsettled and ungrounded, of what is yet to be. In this movement the author's relation to the hero is no longer the relation of subject to object but now takes on an interhuman aspect, where truth rests not on the reality it represents but on intersubjectivity. When the hero becomes I, therefore, so does the author: the one who had made the author other to himself now returns him to himself by turning him over to the realm of spirit. The hero's striving is the striving of the author, who finds success in his art when he realizes that it can have no final outcome.

What Lacan refers to as symbol, then, Bakhtin associates with form and rhythm. With the utterance of "it is finished," the hero does not cease to breathe but takes the longest breath, which is spirit, thereby offering what he has received. Clark and Holquist have described the author Dostoevsky as a Christ to his characters (249), but now it is the hero who assumes that role in relation to his author. If we bear in mind a remark made by Todorov, we see there is no contradiction here: "I can die only for others; conversely, only others can die for me; as Bakhtin has said, 'in all the cemeteries there are only others' " (151). Emerging as *I* from the sepulture of the symbol, the hero consumates his role as other in a movement toward . . . somewhere else. And he takes his author with him.

"The spirit," Lacan has said, "is always somewhere else" (*Language* 34). Lying between—or above—author and hero is the realm of spirit, a third position always elsewhere, into which the soul of the hero is dispersed, beyond the text and the discourse of the author. This third position, however, does not arise at the culmination of a literary work; it is not something achieved. Rather, it is the thing that makes literary discourse possible as a discourse of truth and spirit; it is the origin of the word as the language of the self, the place to which the I returns when, in an act of response, it becomes I. Hence Lacan's accent on Freud's *"Wo es war, soll ich werden.* I must come to the place where that was" (*Écrits* 171). Where it was, I must become, making my *here* the shifting site of dialogical process. "To employ Heideggerian language," Wilden explains, "the 'who' of Dasein is the unanswerable question, whereas the 'where' of Dasein is revealed in almost every word he speaks: the 'who' of Dasein is the shifter 'I,' which is a locus and not a person" (305-6). And the locus of the "who" is the locus of the relation to the Third via the other. But because the Third is always somewhere else, always the *Third*, the movement of return to "where it was" is forever yet to be fulfilled. When the soul of the hero shifts from the category of other to the category of I, it moves from the *is* to the *not yet*, from the relation to the symbol to a relation to truth. As the language of the self, which is a literary language, the word is never what is uttered but what is yet to be uttered, what lies behind or beyond utterance, constituting the relation to the Third.

THE POSITION OF THE THIRD AS OTHER

Heidegger has argued that "in the work of art something other is brought together with the thing that is made" (*Poetry* 19-20). This something other is precisely the Other. What must be shown at this juncture is that the author's relation to the hero or the other requires a relation to a third, to the Other. It must also be pointed out that while Lacan associates the Other with the unconscious, Bakhtin does not use that psychoanalytical term. This difference, of course, opens the door to differences between the two with respect to the ramifications of their concepts of the Other. Nevertheless, we may draw on those concepts to develop further what we have already laid out.

Pursuing our line of thought, then, let it be noted that one way of describing the Third is to say it is the author's implied reader, looking over his shoulder as he engages in his discourse. This implied reader is what distinguishes a work of literature from other texts, for the reader here is not a member of any special interest group or other segment of the population. No, this reader represents the position of the Third or spirit; he is, as we have noted, what Bakhtin terms "the overman, the over-*I*—that is, the witness and judge of every man (of every *I*)" (*Estetika* 342). Lacan expresses a similar idea in "The Subversion of the Subject" when he asserts, "This Other, which is distinguished as the locus of Speech [*parole* or the Word], imposes itself no less as a witness to the Truth" (*Écrits* 305). If, as Lacan claims, "it is by the intersubjectivity of the 'we' which it takes on that the value of a Language as Word is measured" (*Language* 62), the Other is the one who does the measuring and to whom we are accountable for what is measured. Along these lines Bakhtin writes, "Ethical and aesthetic objectification [and therefore justification] requires a profound point of support outside oneself, a profoundly genuine strength, out of which I might truly see myself as other" (*Estetika* 30). It is in the light of the Third, of the Other, that such seeing and shifting from I to other are possible. In short, the Third—what Lacan sometimes regards in terms of the Unconscious—is the origin of consciousness, as Levinas has pointed out: "Consciousness is born as the presence of a third party. . . . It is the entry of the third party, a permanent entry, into the intimacy of the face to face" (*Otherwise* 160). The position of the Third as Other, then, distinguishes the position of the self as one of accountability. The Other is the one who puts the question "Where are you?" to the one whose *where* is continually decided through the word he utters.

To the extent that a language of the self is indeed of the self, it is a language of truth or a language that struggles to give voice to truth. This struggle constitutes the relation to the Third and characterizes the author's relation to the hero. To write the hero is to write the truth witnessed and judged by the Other. Yet, as we have seen, the hero cannot be written. Or rather, as soon as he is written, the author's task is to unwrite him, to release him from the forms of the inscribed. The danger thus reveals itself: if the language of the self is a language of truth, it forever implies one's guilt before the truth. Hence, in Lacan's words, "the spirit that lives as an exile in the creation whose invisible support it is, knows that it is at every instant the master capable of annihilating it" (*Language* 33). If the self lives in the spirit, it is also destroyed by the spirit. As soon as the self speaks itself, it loses itself, and so it must, if it is to find itself again in the movement of the word. Bakhtin, indeed, views the self in such spiritual terms. "Within myself I live in the spirit," he writes. "The spirit is the totality of all meaningful significance and direction in life, of all acts issuing from itself" (*Estetika* 97-98). And so he views the novel, arguing that in the novel the activity is "a spiritual activity of the production and selection of sense, of connections, of axiological relations; it is the inner tension of a spiritual contemplation" (*Esthétique* 79-80). Living within the spirit, I live before the spirit, answerable to the Other for the meaning of my life, for the word and deed that constitute my life in relation to the Other. The spirit is the Other. And the self as spirit is the self who lives in a relation to the Other, which finds its expression in the relation to the other.

We invoke the Other, therefore, in order to introduce to the relation between author and hero, between I and other, the dimension of truth or spirit, which is essential to the language of the self. A similar line of thought turns up in Lacan's concept of the Other. Wilden, in his commentary in *The Language of the Self*, cites a statement by Lacan linking the concept of the Other with the notion of a third position viewed as the realm of truth. "The Other with a big 'O,' " said Lacan, "is the scene of the Word insofar as the scene of the Word is always in third position between two subjects. This is only in order to introduce the dimension of Truth" (269). We must bear in mind here that the "scene of the Word" is always elsewhere and that this "elsewhere" is what makes truth a dimension and not a datum. It is no accident that the language we use to talk about truth in this instance is spatial, as has been the language used to talk about the self. Truth is not something we discover but a relation in which we live. The needful question concerning the spirit is not "What are its attributes?" but "Do I live in relation to this Other that can be deemed a spiritual relation?" Finally, it is not one answer over another that characterizes the position of the Third as Other but the question itself: it is the question that introduces the dimension of truth.

In Bakhtin's essay "The Problem of the Text in Linguistics, Philology, and Other Human Sciences" we find a passage that lends itself to comparison with Lacan's remark above: "Every dialogue proceeds as though against the background of the responsive understanding of a Third who is invisibly present, standing above all the participants in the dialogue" (*Estetika* 306). As a *responsive* understanding, the understanding of the Third is interrogative as well as declarative. Its presence, though invisible, is dialogical—or metadialogical, if you will, since it is the constitutive dimension of every dialogue. For dialogue, by our definition, is the means by which we seek truth. The Other is the one who is there when two are gathered in the unutterable name of truth. He is the one for whom all things are possible, the open horizon of possibility in the word, from which the author voices the possibilities for his hero and for himself. Each voicing of possibility, moreover, is a proliferation of possibility. In the dialogical interchange between author and hero, the discourse of one constantly transforms the discourse of the other, so that the third position shifts; in the words of Bakhtin, "the inner infinity bursts forth and finds no peace" (*Estetika* 179). And each shifting of the Third once again puts the relation of author and hero in question. How does the author free the hero of the confines of form and rhythm? By drawing the hero into a relation to the Third.

We can see, then, that the *who* of the self is inextricably bound to its relation to the Other. One of Lacan's insights from "The Agency of the Letter" comes to mind in this connection: "Who, then, is this other to whom I am more attached than to myself, since, at the heart of my assent to my own identity it is still he who agitates me? . . . This other is the Other" (*Écrits* 172). Reading these lines from Lacan, one cannot help but recall Levinas's statement that "the other in the same determinative of subjectivity is the restlessness of the same disturbed by the other" (*Otherwise* 25). And as soon as Lacan declares this other to be the Other, we are reminded of Levinas's assertion that "the glory of the Infinite reveals itself through what it is capable of doing in the witness" (*Ethics* 109). The inner infinity, the Other at the heart of my own identity, bursts forth as the witness who transforms me into a witness. It has been argued, however, that identity lies more in the *where* than in the *who* of the person. The question that the Other puts to the author and with which he agitates the author is the question that God put to the first man: Where are you? And the author's literary work, his relation to the hero as other, is his answer. As we have seen, the author's presence in the work is rooted in his dialogue with the hero. But this dialogue is also a response to the Other as well as a witnessing of the Other, since the Other is the one who questions the truth of the dialogical relation. The position of the Third as Other is the novel's point of departure and point of return, the place where the novel happens. For the novel is a language of the self.

Although, as Lacan has said, "it is with the appearance of language that the dimension of truth emerges" (*Écrits* 172), the Other as the scene of the word is not simply the atmosphere of language or the historical milieu of the said; to borrow a statement from Bakhtin, "the word is at the same time determined by that which has not been said but which is needed" (*Dialogic* 280). The word, the one thing needful, remains forever unsaid, inviolate, *invisibly* present, present by its absence, present as the trace of an echo that can be heard only as an echo. Once again Levinas's insight comes to mind: "When in the presence of the other I say 'Here I am!', this 'Here I am!' is the place through which the Infinite enters into language, but without giving itself to be seen. Since it is not thematized, in any case originally, it does not appear.

The 'invisible God' is not to be understood as God invisible to the senses, but as God non-thematizable in thought, and nonetheless as non-indifferent to the thought which is not thematization" (*Ethics* 106). What is needed is always nonthematizable in thought or even in language. What is needed is the word, yet it happens that only silence can leave us open for the relation to the Third; it happens that silence speaks. If the Other is the substance of language, he is also the language of silence. The tension between author and hero consists of the silent reverberations of the echoing Other who summons the dialogical relation. In order to create a presence in his hero, the author must become present before the Other. His task in generating a language of the self is to come before the countenance and declare, "Here I am."

Bakhtin expresses this accountability to the Other when he says, "Wherever the alibi becomes a prerequisite for creation and expression there can be no responsibility, no seriousness, no significance. A special responsibility is required . . . ; but this responsibility can be founded only on a profound belief in a higher truth, . . . the belief that another, higher being responds to my special responsibility, that I do not act in an utter void. Apart from this belief there can be only empty pretense" (*Estetika* 179). At the risk of oversimplifying, we have here the suggestion of a difference between artist and artisan, between creation and craft. Creation is always groundless, always free, always an utterance of what is heard in the calling of deep unto deep. "It is from the Other," says Lacan, "that the subject receives even the message he emits" (*Écrits* 305). Here lies the significance of the message: the Other, who responds to my special responsibility, makes a messenger of me. I may flee to alibi, but I cannot refuse; I cannot slip away. The most common form of alibi in this case is the designated or predetermined audience *named* as a particular interest group. Only when the implied reader is the nameless, nonthematizable Third, the witness and judge of every human being, does the author operate within "the categories of purpose and meaning," the categories of the literary. The Other is always in a Third position because he is always higher, eternally more, forever on the other side of discourse: the spirit is always somewhere else. The relation to spirit, therefore, requires one responsibility *more*, and I forever fall short. The author (I) draws nigh to the Other by becoming the

self he is summoned to become through his dialogical relation to
the hero (other); the author draws nigh by virtue of his special
responsibility.

Yet as he nears the Other, the difference that distinguishes the
higher becomes even more pronounced, and the Other recedes;
once again the question is put to the author and he is summoned to
respond. Once again, approaching the position of the hero as
other, the author must become other in order to approach the *not
yet* to which the Other beckons him. The debt increases in the
measure it is paid; the more I answer, the greater my responsibility. It is in this light that we must understand Lacan when he
says:

> How would the Word, in fact, be able to exhaust the sense of
> the Word or, to put it better, with the Oxford logical
> positivists, the meaning of meaning—except in the act which
> engenders it? Thus Goethe's reversal of its presence at the
> origin of things, "In the beginning was the action," is itself
> reversed in its turn: it was certainly the *verbe* that was in the
> beginning, and we live in its creation, but it is the action of
> our spirit which continues that creation by constantly renew-
> ing it. And we can only turn back on that action by letting
> ourselves constantly be pushed further ahead by it. [*Language*
> 34-35]

Yet we are not exactly pushed ahead—we are summoned forth,
called upon to respond. Responsibility thus entails repetition. The
revelation of difference is a discovery of a loss or a lack and
demands nonindifference; the self, indeed, is precisely difference
transformed into nonindifference through the dialogical relation
to the Other. For the author, this relation, again, finds its expression in his relation to the hero. It is in the light of his responsibility
to the Other that the author's relation to the hero is a relation of
difference that is nonindifference. "Living through the sufferings
of another," Bakhtin writes, "I experience them precisely as *his*
sufferings, in the category of the *other*, and my reaction to him is not
a cry of pain but a word of comfort and a helping hand" (*Estetika*
25-26). The relation between author and hero is similar, and this is
Bakhtin's point. The nonindifference issuing from the higher re-

sponsibility is what makes the word as the language of the self an offering of the self. It may be associated with what Bakhtin calls intention when he says that the word "becomes 'one's own' only when the speaker populates it with his own intention" (*Dialogic* 293). For to populate the word with one's own intention is to instill it with one's own self.

Bakhtin's "profound belief in a higher truth" is impossible without intention, intensity, passion—impossible without the *loving* consciousness Bakhtin invokes in "Author and Hero" when he asserts, "The soul is spirit unrealized for itself, reflected in the loving consciousness of another (person, God)" (*Estetika* 98). We are not speaking of any feeling here. Feelings are in us, while we live in the love between I and the other, between I and the Third. If the word is spirit, it is also love. Where Bakhtin writes, "person, God," we may read "hero, Other," who combine in their relation to the author to make his soul or self something unrealized but continually in the process of realization. The *literary* endeavor is defined by the presence of and responsibility to the Other as implied reader, and it is love that posits the Other. While some may point out that, unlike Bakhtin, Lacan does not speak in such spiritual or religious terms, Bakhtin's claim has its similarities with Lacan's thinking. For in "The Subversion of the Subject" we read, "I can only just prove to the Other that he exists, not, of course, with the proofs for the existence of God, with which over the centuries he has been killed off, but by loving him" (*Écrits* 317). Although—or because—the author undertakes his literary creation in the shadow of death, he also moves by the light of love. Like the motif of the double, love is not only a prevalent theme in literature but is the thing that characterizes the literary project itself. There, where author, hero, and the Third—I, other, and the Other—move in the name of love, literature happens. And so does the self.

Having examined the relation between author and hero, we find that the language of the self lies not in the said but in the process of saying. At the silent threshold of saying, the word that is the language of the self comes from the human being and from beyond him in a summons that is heard in the act of response. Here, in the words of Levinas, "a silence resounds about what has been muffled, the silence of the parcelling out of being, by which entities in their identities are illuminated and show themselves" (*Otherwise* 38). Because the self is forever yet to be decided in the tension of summons and response, it is not subject to thematization or categorization. The I of the author is continually shifting in his effort to become other and thus bring his hero—and himself—to life. This struggle entails all the drama of signification, of the I-for-the-other who responds to the Third or to truth. It is not simply a matter of generating signs but of becoming a sign, or a self as sign: the self is the language of itself.

But there is one more point to be made. In our reaction to author and hero, we bear the same responsibility to the Other that calls the author to his own endeavor. His offering of himself to his hero is in turn an offering to us, for the sake of us. Here the Other is in a third position between the critic as I and the author as other. "Beginning with any text," Bakhtin has pointed out, "we always arrive . . . at the human voice, which is to say we come up against the human being" (*Dialogic* 252-53); thus, he goes on to say, "the work and the world represented in it enter the real world and enrich it, and the real world enters the work and its world as part of the process of its creation, as well as part of its subsequent life, in a continual renewing of the work through the creative perception of listeners and readers" (254). Ellie Ragland-Sullivan makes a similar observation relative to Lacan: "Within a Lacanian worldview, there can be no rational, classical, objective reader who approaches a text which is a discrete, contained, and separate entity, for each was structured by the language surrounding it and each will operate its own linguistic possibilities on the other in an intersubjective dialectic" (570).

Our response to the text, therefore, takes on a literary or creative dimension of its own. If our relation to the author is to be an expression of our relation to the Other, then we must become other, changed by our dialogue with the literary text. "What can guarantee the inner bonding of the elements of personality?" Bakhtin asks. "Only the wholeness of responsibility. With my life I must answer for what I have experienced and understood in art. . . . Art and life are not one and the same, but they must become one within me in the wholeness of my responsibility" (*Estetika* 5-6). There, in the "I must answer," lies our spiritual life.

Thus the author's verbal art teaches us the art of becoming, the art of the word as the language of the self. When art and life do not become one in the wholeness of my responsibility—when criticism is confined to explication and commentary—I lose the word and with it my self and soul. We can see, then, why Emerson describes Bakhtin's "huge text"—*Problems of Dostoevsky's Poetics*—as "a basically religious quest into the nature of the Word" (Preface xxxi). That a person might become an author who creates a hero in the face of the Third is a religious phenomenon. It points up the religious dimension of literature, of the language of the self, and of our stake in both.

Thus we come to a turning point at which the relation between literature and spirit may become more clear. We see, for example, that the involvement of laughter and madness with the utterly alien, as discussed in the first essay, has a bearing on the relation to the Other that guides the creation of literature. We see further that the poetics of spirit examined in the second essay implicates the self's relation and responsibility to the Third. It is time now to pursue what has already been implied through our frequent citation of Levinas. Although the accent so far has been on literature, we shall now shift the emphasis to spirit, crossing the bridge of signification and responsibility. In doing so, we may see some of the reasons behind Clark and Holquist's claim that "Bakhtin's distinctiveness consists in his invention of a philosophy of language that has immediate application not only to linguistics and stylistics but also to the most urgent concerns of everyday life" (9). Let us proceed, then, to our consideration of Bakhtin and Levinas and explore those most urgent concerns of everyday life, which are the concerns of the spirit.

FOUR

Bakhtin and Levinas

Signification, Responsibility, Spirit

Mikhail Bakhtin is known primarily for his theories on literature. But since those theories rest largely on a concept of dialogical discourse, his ideas have implications for how we view the word and its role in human interrelations. "His accent is on the *Zwischenwelt*," as Clark and Holquist put it, "or the world between consciousnesses" (9). Bakhtin insists, for example, that "language, for the individual consciousness, lies on the border between oneself and the other" (*Dialogic* 293). And Voloshinov states, "In essence, the *word is a two-sided* act. It is determined equally by *whose* word it is and by *whom* it is for. As a word, it is precisely the *product* of the *interrelation between speaker and listener*" (*Marksizm* 87).

In these remarks alone questions arise concerning the connection between the signifying function of the word and the activity of listening and response. What, for instance, do we learn about signification from the fact that *I* am the one responding to *this* human being? What does *my* significance, my meaning, have to do with my ability to respond, with my responsibility? And how is my life involved with the life of the word that unfolds in the dialogical relation to the other? Questions such as these provide a basis for a comparison of Bakhtin with Emmanuel Levinas; Clark and Holquist, in fact, place Bakhtin in "a tradition of thinkers from Heraclitus to Emmanuel Levinas, who have preferred the powers that inhere in the centrifugal forces" (8).

Levinas, a Lithuanian-born French thinker, approaches signification and subjectivity in terms of response and responsibility. In *Otherwise than Being*, the work of particular interest to the investigation at hand, he asserts, "All my inwardness is invested in the form of a despite-me, for-another. Despite-me, for another, is signification par excellence. And it is the sense of the 'oneself,' that accusative that derives from no nominative; it is the very fact of finding oneself while losing oneself" (11). This "despite-me, for-another," suggestive of what Clark and Holquist call "centrifugal forces," is the substance of responsibility, which is also a vulnerability. On Levinas's view, my significance is rooted in a signification for the other expressed through the offering of myself to the other. "I can enjoy and suffer by the other," he says later in the same work, "only because I am-for-the-other, am signification, because the contact with skin is still a proximity of face, a responsibility, an obsession with the other, being one-for-the-other, which is the very birth of *signification* beyond *being*" (90). In Levinas's language, "beyond being" means beyond thematization and generalization. I am unique and irreplaceable in my proximity to the other, which defines my significance for the other. No one and nothing else can assume my responsibility or offer the word and the self that are mine to offer.

But who or what summons the offering? According to Levinas, it is the infinite "imprinting itself as a trace" and "showing itself as a Responsibility-for-the-Other," which is prior to any acceptance or refusal of responsibility ("Signature" 189; Levinas's capitalized word "Other" does not refer to the Third or to Lacan's Other but to what we have been calling the *other,* with a small *o*). Beckoning me, "as when one says: 'Someone is asking for you' " (*Ethics* 98), the trace of the Infinite in the face of the other calls upon me "to say: here I am. To do something for the Other. To give. To be human spirit, that's it. This incarnation of human subjectivity guarantees its spirituality" (*Ethics* 97). Like Levinas, Bakhtin considers the relation to the other human being to be "not merely a moral imperative," as Clark and Holquist point out, "but an epistemological requirement" (208). Bakhtin, like Levinas, has a sense of something beyond, something otherwise, which underlies my responsibility to the other and the significance of my expression. "A special responsibility is required," he declares. "But this responsibility can be founded only on a profound belief in a higher truth, . . . the belief that another, higher being responds to my special responsibility, that I do not act in an utter void. Apart from this belief there can be only empty pretense" (*Estetika* 179). What

Levinas associates with the Infinite or the "otherwise than being" and what Bakhtin views in terms of a higher being we shall here regard as spirit. The spirit is the one who summons us to respond and who is revealed in our response, in the signification of the I-for-the-other.

The ensuing comparison of Bakhtin and Levinas will show that there is no signification without responsibility and that the spiritual life of a human being—his living in the spirit—lies in responsibility. Signification is the saying of the word; the saying of the word is the offering of the self; and the offering of the self is the opening of the spirit. Meaning is grounded in signification and is born in a response to the question that arises from the spirit between myself and the other: Where are you? And my answer is the offering of myself to the other. Let us now consider this event of offering which consists of signification, responsibility, and spirit.

SIGNIFICATION: THE LIVING WORD

In *Problems of Dostoevsky's Poetics* Bakhtin argues that the word "never gravitates toward a single consciousness or a single voice. The life of the word is contained in its transfer from one mouth to another, from one context to another context" (202). The word is never in a context, but rather the context is in the word; it is defined by the from-here-to-here that distinguishes the transfer of the word. The word creates the context, shapes the mouth, in an act of creation in which "what is called into being answers to a call that could not have reached it, since, brought out of nothingness, it obeys before hearing the order" (Levinas, *Otherwise* 113). The word is never object but always subject, summoned in its summons, not a thing or a principle or a sound but a force. Thus we see the error of Saussurian and formalist or structuralist views of language as a system of signification. Signification is not a static set of points or an organization of signs but a movement, a shift, from one to the other. We must also note that the movement Bakhtin describes is a movement from mouth to mouth, not from mouth to ear; speaking and listening are simultaneous, not mutually exclusive. The organ by which we hear is the tongue; whether we are in the position of speaker or listener, we hear by responding. Heidegger's statement in *Poetry, Language, Thought* readily comes to mind: "Language speaks. Man speaks in that he responds to language. This responding is a hearing" (210). Bakhtin makes this point in *Aesthetics of Verbal Art* when he says, "Every understanding of living speech, of living expression, bears an actively responsive character. . . . The speaker himself is situated in precisely such an actively responsive understanding" (*Estetika* 246-47). Just as there is no smile without a face, so is there no understanding without speaking. Signification lies in the activity, in the actively responsive character, of speaking and listening. Sense is *born*, like a new life, from this responsive interaction. The word exacts something from us. It has meaning to the extent that we make it an offering, whether as speaker or listener. And the offering is the self.

In signification, in the life of the word, the offering of the one to the other is always a "tearing away from oneself," as Levinas puts it: "Giving has meaning only as tearing away from oneself despite oneself, and not only *without* me. And to be torn from oneself despite oneself has meaning only as a being torn from the complacency in oneself characteristic of enjoyment, snatching the bread from one's mouth. Only a subject that eats can be for-the-other, or can signify. Signification, the one-for-the-other, has meaning only among beings of flesh and blood" (*Otherwise* 74). All signification associated with the living word is eucharistic. There is but one bread, one body, one life. As we eat, so are we bonded, one for the other and in the other; as we are bonded, so we live. But the living bond, the living word, lives only in the offering of what bonds: we have only as much life as we offer up, only as much self as we tear away. We are not what we eat; rather, we are what we snatch from our mouths for the other to eat. This is where we are led by Bakhtin's insight that the word lives in the transfer from mouth to mouth: it lives in the tearing of the self from itself. Signification arises, therefore, only in the self-signification of vulnerability. Exposition is exposure: we know ourselves by our wounds. It is from those wounds that meaning flows; there is no other deliverance of the imprisoned sense. What happens when the word becomes flesh? It bleeds. For it is by the wounds that we recognize the absolute difference that calls for signification; signification is an answer to the outcry of one who bleeds when pricked. And he who bleeds always bleeds for me.

In vulnerability, then, we encounter the noncoincidence of the one and the other, of this and that, from which emerges the problem of identity and of self. "A man never coincides with himself," Bakhtin observes. "One cannot apply to him the formula $A = A$. . . . The genuine life of the personality takes place at the point of non-coincidence between a man and himself" (*Problems* 59). Why? Because this is where the genuine life of the word, of signification, takes place. Recall what Levinas says in this connection: "Signification is the one-for-the-other which characterizes an identity that does not coincide with itself. This is in fact all the gravity of an animate body, that is, one offered to another, expressed or opened up! This opening up, like a reverse *conatus*, an inversion of essence, is a relationship across an absolute difference" (*Otherwise* 70). The formula $A = A$ characterizes the self-coincidence of complacent self-indulgence. It is true that a man never coincides with himself—as long as he is a man, a human being; that is to say, as long as he lives in the I-Thou relation of dialogue. Slipping, however, into the monological sleep of the dative case—into an existence ruled by "to me" and "for me"—he becomes an It equal to himself, a zero equal to zero, closed in on himself. The one-for-the-other of signification, on the other hand, is an identity not identical to itself, at once more and less than itself. If turned back upon itself, the enclosure of the circle becomes the exposure of the Möbius strip, its inside opened up to the outside, of a piece with its outside, the inside *for* the outside. "My body is a fundamentally inner body," says Bakhtin. "The body of the other is a fundamentally outer body" (*Estetika* 44). This is the absolute difference traversed in the inversions of signification. Hence in its transfer from mouth to mouth and in its rejoinder within that transfer, the word announces the profound incongruity in correspondence. As it is torn from one mouth, like a piece of bread, and offered to the other, the word reveals the one-for-the-other of absolute difference.

Bakhtin stresses the significance of the revelation of difference in his essay "Forms of Time and of the Chronotope in the Novel," arguing that where there is discourse, there is encounter. For discourse, or the word, announces the difference that makes encounter possible, even—or especially—encounter with oneself. Discourse is the road through the other that leads to oneself: the living word is the way, the place, and time of encounter. Thus

Bakhtin observes that "the importance of the chronotope of the road in literature is immense. . . . The motif of meeting is combined with other motifs, for example that of apparition ('epiphany') in the religious realm" (*Dialogic* 98-99). The chronotope should not be viewed as a coordinate in space and time but as a node or nexus in discourse where space and time are generated by the gravity of the eye-to-eye, depth-to-depth encounter. If signification consists of a transfer of the word from mouth to mouth, it also lies in the meeting of the one and the other face-to-face. The "dead pan" face is the wordless face. The face comes to life with utterance born of encounter. The living word enlivens it by revealing the trace of something more that distinguishes the face, the trace of its past and of the countenance that summons us to our own present. Levinas helps us to see this point in a statement that sheds additional light on Bakhtin's remark about the chronotope of the road. "The epiphany," writes Levinas, "of that which can present itself directly, outwardly and eminently—is *visage*. The expressing helps the expression here, brings help to itself, signifies, speaks. The revelation of the face is language" ("Signature" 185). The face is made of expression, and expression consists of language. The look on the face, the vision of the visage, addresses the listening eye. If the word lives in transfer, transfer lives in the face.

In *Ethics and Infinity* Levinas says more: "The face is signification, and signification without a context. . . . All signification in the usual sense of the term is relative to a context: the meaning of something is in its relation to another thing. Here, to the contrary, the face is meaning all by itself. You are you. In this sense one can say that the face is not 'seen.' It is what cannot become a content, which your thought would embrace; it is uncontainable, it leads you beyond" (86-87). The face is I Am That I Am: meaning all by itself. When we hear a poet cry, "The old man, the child, and the stranger all call for me," we do not have to ask which old man or when or where in order to understand. The living word lives in its curious equation to itself, which is also a noncoincidence with itself. It is the equation and difference of summons and response: tell them I Am has sent you. At first glance it may seem that Levinas's idea stands in contradiction to Bakhtin's claim that "the life of the word is contained in its transfer . . . from one context to another context" (*Problems* 202), but a second look will show that such is not the case. The space between contexts is without context, and this is where the face makes its appearance. It is the creator of context, the flesh of the word that places us *in situation*. It draws us to the threshold of the beyond, which, Bakhtin notes, "can be combined with the motif of the encounter, but its most fundamental instance is as the chronotope of *crisis* and *break* in a life" (*Dialogic* 248). The face is signification because the face, uncontainable, is a break in the life of the one, summoning the one to be for the other. The crisis or break announces the absolute difference that establishes the transfer of the word. Unless the face is signification without context, there can be no noncoincidence between a human being and himself.

The face appears at the threshold, where the one encounters the other face-to-face. This "face-to-face" is an implication of the one in the other, a face meeting another face, which characterizes signification. And in signification, implication means summons, or what Levinas calls assignation: "The implication of the one in the other signifies the assignation of the one by the other. This assignation is the very signifyingness of signification, or the psyche of the soul. Through the psyche proximity is my approaching of the other, the fact that the proximity of the same and the other is never close enough. The summoned one is the ego—me" (*Otherwise* 137). A remark in Voloshinov's *Marxism and the Philosophy of Language* immediately comes to mind: "By the very nature of its existence, the subjective psyche is localized somewhere between the organism and the outside world, somewhere *on the border* between these two spheres of reality" (*Marksizm* 29). What Bakhtin refers to above as transfer, Levinas describes as approach. In either case we are concerned with movement or process, and that is why the human being never coincides with himself, is never here but always there, not *Hier*sein but *Da*sein. The assignation of the one by the other is the "signifyingness of signification" because the assignation is the transmittal of a message. Signification is meaning, and meaning is message. In the transfer by which the word lives, the other transforms the one into a messenger and a witness who must draw near by going forth. The psyche is the realization of the difference, and therefore of the distance, that makes proximity a matter of approaching rather than anchoring. Never close enough, I am always guilty: the word *I* is a confession. The summoned one is thus summoned with a question: Where are you? Which means: Where are you going; what do you signify? Signification, the living word, is always something called forth and called for, itself calling itself. And it finds its breath in the open air of the yet-to-be.

Hence we hear Bakhtin assert, "Forming itself in an atmosphere of the already spoken, the word is at the same time determined by that which has not been said but which is needed" (*Dialogic* 280). The word is formed at the threshold, not simply on this side but from the thither side of the said, where the trace of what is needed is not the fading trace of what has been but of what shall have been. What is needed, then, is not something more to be added to what has been said but the process of saying itself, in which, in Levinas's words, "the subject of saying does not give signs, it becomes a sign, turns into an allegiance" (*Otherwise* 49). To become a messenger is to become a sign: this is the as-sign-ation made manifest through the trace of the needful in the face. Saying, therefore, "is already a sign made to another," Levinas goes on to state, "a sign of this giving of signs, that is, of this non-indifference, a sign of this impossibility of slipping away and being replaced, of this identity, this uniqueness: here I am" (145). I am the one who cannot turn his face from the face. Because I live in the word, even my effort to turn away is a sign of this giving of signs; even in my flight I become a sign. In signification, moreover, the absolute difference becomes a nonindifference not through what is said but through the act of saying, whereby I go forth as I am called forth. As Levinas points out, " 'Here I am!' means 'Send me' " (*Otherwise* 199; cf. Isaiah 6:8). In this offering of oneself as a sign the soul is born, "given not as a thing," Bakhtin notes, "but only in signifying expression" (*Estetika* 284). With the soul is born the living word and from the living word the soul: the soul is signification without context, the thing that is sent in the transfer from mouth to mouth.

At this juncture we must make more clear a distinction already suggested, the distinction between the living word and words or language, between saying and the said. Bakhtin and Levinas, indeed, have similar ideas along these lines. We have cited Bakhtin's statement that the word forms "itself in an atmosphere of the already spoken" (*Dialogic* 280). Levinas, however, pursues this idea a bit further: "A word is a nomination, as much as a denomination, a consecrating of the 'this as this' or 'this as that' by a saying which is also *understanding* and *listening*, absorbed in the said. . . . The said, the word, is not simply a sign of a meaning, nor even only an *expression* of a meaning; the word at once pro-claims and establishes an identification of this with that in the *already said*" (*Otherwise* 36-37). Reading these lines, we recall Bakhtin's position that the word is determined not only by what has been said but by what is needed, for listening and understand-ing belong to what is needed. As suggested from the beginning of this section, the notion of transfer is at work: this carried over to that, saying over to understanding, proclamation over to identi-fication. The movement is perhaps not so much from here to there as it is a movement at the spot, as in hearing oneself speak. "The dif-ference is itself the stillness," Heidegger expresses it. "The dif-ference is the bidder" (*Poetry* 207). Emerging out of the "dif-fer-ence," which is a process of one thing referring itself to another, the word changes what it situates and undoes what it settles; it is never the same at the end of its utterance as at the beginning. "The word already spoken," Bakhtin tells us, "has a ring of hopelessness in its already having been uttered: the word uttered is the dead flesh of meaning" (*Estetika* 117).

It is true: the word is not simply an expression of meaning—it is an alteration of meaning. Here lies its life and its power of sig-nification; signification is transformation. It is the consecration of this as that, an absorption or transfer of saying into the said—the living word into words. There is no signification outside of death, a point that Lacan helps us to see when he says, "There where it was just now, there where it was for a while, between an extinction that is still glowing and a birth that is retarded, 'I' can come into being and disappear from what I say" (*Écrits* 300). And because saying disappears into the said, signification always implies a meaning beyond what comes to us in signs. It is verbal and is rather like the verb Foucault describes when he says, "The threshold of language lies at the point where the verb first appears. This verb must therefore be treated as a composite entity, at the same time a word among other words, . . . and yet set apart from all other words, in a region which is not that of the spoken, but rather that from which one speaks. It is on the fringe of discourse, at the connection between what is said and what is saying itself, exactly at the point where signs are in the process of becoming language" (*Order* 93). Signification implies rebirth: there is no signification outside of resurrection.

We may now better understand Clark and Holquist's insight into Bakhtin's concept of signification, an insight expressed when, citing Voloshinov's *Marxism and the Philosophy of Language*, they explain, "The Bakhtinian myth of significance is thus a story of a dying and reviving God: 'meaning—an abstract, self-identical element—is subsumed under the theme and torn apart by the theme's living contradictions so as to return in the shape of a new meaning with a fixity and self-identity only for the while, just as it had before" (*Marksizm* 232). Nothing has its life except by the living word—and that is why all things must die. Yet as they perish, so are they reborn, like a grain of wheat that falls to the ground and dies to bring forth fruit. Thus saying is forever called for, the I forever called forth; what is needed remains a determinant of words, and the living word remains open-ended, unfinalized, tensed at the entrance of the tomb, about to proclaim and establish an identification of this with that. The living word is the "holding open of openness" Levinas describes when he declares, "Saying is this passivity of passivity and this dedication to the other, this sincerity. Not the communication of a said, which would immediately cover over and extinguish or absorb the said, but saying holding open its openness, without excuses, evasions or alibis, delivering itself without saying anything said" (*Otherwise* 143). Recalling Bakhtin's assertion that the word is one's own "only when the speaker populates it with his own intention" (*Dialogic* 293), we now see that intention is to be understood in terms of the speaker's relation to the other. It is the thing that opens the one *for* the other, aglow on the edge of utterance. Again, signification is not simply communication; viewed according to the living word, it is the open-endedness of a saying that is both already past and yet to be, continually calling forth and called for.

To live in the word and before the face, therefore, is to live in ongoing response. The categories of signification, of purpose and meaning, are "the categories of the not-yet-existing," to use Bakhtin's phrase (*Estetika* 109). Meaning, on this view, does not lie in speculation or contemplation but in the offering of the soul through the saying of the soul in an act of response to the other.

Meaning means having one responsibility *more*. In this regard Levinas claims, "The *saying* is the fact that before the face I do not simply remain there contemplating it, I respond to it. The saying is a way of greeting the Other, but to greet the Other is already to answer for him. It is difficult to be silent in someone's presence; this difficulty has its ultimate foundation in this signification proper to the saying, whatever is the said" (*Ethics* 88). The living word lives before the face. Signification does not happen within a chain of signifiers; rather, it occurs before the face. Further, if saying is a way of greeting the other, then it is an affirmation of having heard the other even before anything has been said. Levinas quotes Isaiah 65:24, "Before they call, I will answer," insisting that "the formula is to be taken literally" (*Otherwise* 150). The word lives antecedently, and my greeting the other is an acknowledgment of my responsibility to and for the other, of my antecedent responsibility. It is difficult to remain silent before the face because from the beyond of that silence—from a past outside of any *was* and a future always yet to be—issues the summons to respond, to take on significance through signification.

The summons that arises from the difference between me and the other, moreover, makes the relation of difference a relation of nonindifference. "The difference in proximity between the one and the other," Levinas explains, "between me and a neighbor, turns into non-indifference, precisely into my responsibility. Non-indifference, humanity, the-one-for-the-other is the very signifyingness of signification" (*Otherwise* 166). As we have seen, proximity is approach: to be before the face, in proximity, is to be in motion. To be face-to-face is to be faced with difference: each face is unique unto itself. This must be kept in mind when we read Clark and Holquist's statement that Bakhtin "conceives the old problem of identity along the lines not of 'the same as' but of 'simultaneous with' " (9-10). This uniqueness of time is what establishes the spatiality of difference; it creates the here and there of responsive relation, which is precisely nonindifference. The "signifyingness" of signification is its dialogical dimension. In the lines above, then, Levinas makes explicit what has been implicit throughout this discussion of signification. The activity of response characteristic of signification turns on an assignation and an ability to respond, on responsibility; signification, in short, is dialogical relation. To address signification is to address the responsibility revealed in dialogical relation.

RESPONSIBILITY: THE DIALOGICAL RELATION

In an early essay titled "Art and Responsibility" (1920), Bakhtin raises a question: What can guarantee the inner bonding of the elements of personality? And he answers, "Only the whole-ness of responsibility" (*Estetika* 5). Later on, in *Problems of Dos-toevsky's Poetics*, he adds something to that statement that may add to our understanding of it: "The genuine life of the personality is made available only through a *dialogic* penetration of that person-ality" (59). But "made available" is not quite the proper phrasing; it is not as if something is brought out of hiding. Rather, the genuine life is brought into being, is born in dialogical penetration. The substance and significance of the subjective psyche is estab-lished in the responsibility that distinguishes dialogical relation. The distance or difference that initially isolates me from the other also isolates me from myself. So isolated, I am fragmented, either paralyzed by monological mimicry or muted by a fear of vul-nerability. The entry into dialogue is the opening up of what had thus been interred. To engage in dialogue is to assume respon-sibility in the way a novel, for example, assumes a form, answering to and for the other. I am able to penetrate and thus substantiate myself only by way of the other. Hence one does not imply two; two, rather, are necessary to constitute the wholeness of one. The outer relation is the basis of the inner bonding, yet within that relation the inner/outer, subject/object, I/other distinctions col-lapse: the wholeness of one is the oneness of the whole.

This line of thought is what leads Levinas to assert, "Subjec-tivity is the other in the same. . . . The other in the same deter-minative of subjectivity is the restlessness of the same disturbed by the other" (*Otherwise* 25). Subjectivity is not solipsistic isolation but dialogical relation. Subjectivity is responsibility; conscious-ness is restlessness. The disturbance Levinas refers to is the sum-mons that comes from the other and from beyond him; it is the Thou shaking the I from its deadly sleep, the sleep of indifference that turns the I into an It, the sleep of Peter in Gethsemane. Only in wakefulness can I utter the needful "Here I am" that constitutes my presence before the countenance. Only in wakefulness can I take on the responsibility within the dialogical relation that determines who I am. The other's disturbance or awakening of the same, it must be noted, is not only an opening of the eye but also an opening of a wound; this is the dialogical penetration. I must rend myself, tear away from myself in a tearing open, and expose myself to being wounded. Only in this way do I move out of myself and into the dialogical relation where the other moves into me and where signification thus occurs. If "signification is witness or martyrdom," as Levinas claims (*Otherwise* 78), so too is subjectivity; so too is responsibility. Responding to the Thou, I become I; becoming I, I am wounded. "The other calls upon that sensibility with a vocation that wounds," we read in *Otherwise than Being*, "calls upon an irrevocable responsibility, and thus the very identity of a subject" (77-78). And this calling is a joining, a summons to be made whole. In Heidegger's helpful words, "pain is the joining agent in the rending that divides and gathers. Pain is the joining of the rift. The joining is the threshold. It settles the between, the middle of the two that are separated in it. Pain joins the rift of the dif-ference. Pain is the dif-ference itself" (*Poetry* 204). The other asks, "Where are you?" And I answer with my wounds.

He who is not wounded, then, is guilty, and guilt is our distance and difference from the other that single us out as the one whose response is summoned. Thus Heidegger describes resolve as "the calling-forth-of-oneself to one's ownmost being-guilty" (*Sein* 305). "Only error individualizes," as Bakhtin puts it (*Problems* 81). And this point brings us back to the face. "A face is a trace of itself," says Levinas, "given over to my responsibility, but to which I am wanting and faulty. It is as though I were responsible for his mortality, and guilty for surviving" (*Otherwise* 91). The guilty one is the one without wounds. My fault is that I have not opened up enough for the other to enter the same; my fault is that I am not the dialogical I who is for the other. Offering myself up in the dialogical relation, then, is my one avenue of redemption. Yet the thing that distinguishes the dialogical relation is that every word calls for a reply. "The more I answer the more I am responsible," Levinas points out. "The more I approach the neighbor with whom I am encharged the further away I am" (*Otherwise* 93). The debt increases in the measure that it is paid; the distance and difference grow more pronounced with their acknowledgment. The greater my awareness of the scope of responsibility, the more I realize my failure to meet that responsibility. The response not only answers a call but itself calls for an answer; the affirmation is a confession, the revelation an indictment. What Bakhtin says in *Problems of Dostoevsky's Poetics* is true: "Only in communion, in the interaction of one person with another, can the 'man in man' be revealed" (252). For the "man in man" is the man in debt, the man who must answer all the more as he answers. He is the self who, just because he is a *self*, is guilty, faced with the project of eternal expiation.

The dialogical relation thus implies a relation to the infinite, which is a relation to spirit. But we shall examine this point in detail below. For now let it be noted that responsibility brings us to the edge of an abyss that grows deeper as we approach it, looming before us and cutting into us. This proximity with the boundless is a proximity with the other that, Levinas tells us, "is quite distinct from every other relationship, and has to be conceived as a responsibility for the other; it might be called humanity, or subjectivity, or self" (*Otherwise* 46). If the dialogical word is the language of the self, then it is the language for the other, the language of the one-for-the-other; in short, it is the language of responsibility and signification. To say that the self is responsible for the other, then, is to declare that the self is signification. Living in the categories of purpose and meaning, my I-for-myself is transformed into I-for-the-other. If identity is rendered in terms of those marks of distinction that isolate the self from the other, then the self is the opposite of its identity, its *is* standing over against its *not yet*. There is nothing of the self, nothing of significance, in ID cards, licenses, diplomas, or credentials; these are soporifics with which we maintain our sleep and our illusions. In the realm of responsibility, it is the other that distinguishes the self, and that realm is the dialogical relation, where the other in the same makes the same other to himself.

Thus we can see why Levinas writes, "In the form of responsibility, the psyche in the soul is the other in me, a malady of identity, both accused and *self*, the same for the other, the same by the other" (*Otherwise* 69). Responsibility is the form of the psyche in the soul, the other in me that makes me other to myself. Only by becoming other to myself can I become for-the-other. To be a self within the dialogical relation of responsibility is to incur this malady of identity. But if, as Bakhtin claims, the relation to the other is "the moment of man's limitation in the world" (*Estetika* 34), it is also the moment of his exaltation. Clark and Holquist, in fact, point out an important contrast between Freud and Bakhtin on this point, explaining that "in Freud, the more of the other, the less of the self; in Bakthin, the more of the other, the more of the self" (206). The more of the other, the more substance within the self: the abyss that cuts into me gives me depth. Levinas has understood in this connection that "the proximity of the neighbor in its trauma does not only strike up against me, but exalts and elevates me, and, in the literal sense of the term, inspires me. Inspiration, heteronomy, is the very pneuma of the psyche. Freedom is borne by the responsibility it could not shoulder, an elevation and inspiration without complacency" (*Otherwise* 124). Freedom occurs, in other words, when the limitation posed by the other leads me to penetrate my own limits within the relation to the other; to be free is to be free *for* the other, not free *of* the other. The breath upon which the other's word vibrates is the breath that breathes life into me; as I am inspired, so do I respire, so do I respond. What Levinas recognizes as heteronomy, moreover, Bakhtin sees as the heteroglossia by which "languages are dialogically implicated *in* each other and begin to exist *for* each other" (*Dialogic* 400). And the languages in this case are those of the same and of the other that constitute the dialogical relation.

The trauma of "striking up against" that Levinas refers to, then, occurs in the dialogical offering and receiving of the word, in signification. "Subjectivity," in Levinas's words, "is being thrown back on oneself" (*Otherwise* 112), because subjectivity is the dialogical penetration of the self through the trauma and the wounds suffered in response to the other and in answering for the other. Through those wounds the other enters the same; this entering is inspiration, and inspiration is the psyche or the soul. To be chosen is to be chosen for suffering. To be a living subject is to be subjected. "In the exposure to wounds and outrages," says Levinas, "in the feeling proper to responsibility, the oneself is provoked as irreplaceable, as devoted to the other, without being able to resign, and thus as incarnated in order to offer itself, to suffer and to give" (*Otherwise* 105). No one can answer in my place any more than another can die in my place. This predetermination of responsibility is what constitutes our freedom. Incarnation is signification, and signification is destiny, not as something that molds us but as something that summons our response. This constant calling is what makes responsibility a persecution free of alienation, for it instills the human being with "*something that only he himself can reveal, in a free act of self-consciousness and discourse*," to borrow a phrase from Bakhtin (*Problems* 58). In brief, responsibility gives us a face, a cheek to turn, by which we stand face-to-face in dialogical relation.

Levinas, in fact, makes a noteworthy observation in this connection: "Face and discourse are tied. The face speaks. It speaks, it is in this that it renders possible and begins all discourse. I have just refused the notion of vision to describe the authentic relationship with the Other; it is discourse and, more exactly, response or responsibility which is this authentic relationship" (*Ethics* 87–88). The authentic relationship is dialogical relation. Within such relation the face is never seen, the word never heard. What is seen is the flesh of the word; what is heard is the response to the word. Word and face are of a piece. The other's word is the other's face, the thing exposed to me, summoning my own exposure, my own word. Like a hungry child, the other pleas for me to behold his face and thus receive his word; and in order to receive his word, I must respond to it: I must show my face. "Exposedness is the one-in-responsibility," as Levinas expresses it (*Otherwise* 56). The one in responsibility falls under the eye of the other, turned inside out in the recognition of the other that comes with response. Bakhtin has remarked, "Having looked upon ourselves through the eyes of another, we continually return to ourselves throughout life" (*Estetika* 17); but this is not precisely the case, unless he has in mind something expressed and thus heard through the eyes of the other. In any case, it is true that there is no response to the other without a return to oneself, for there is no responding to the other without being made other to oneself. From those eyes, from that face, comes the assignation that returns us to the inside of ourselves as the one called upon to respond. Thus seen, we are exposed. One is never naked alone; nakedness is always before the other.

This is what it means to say, as Bakhtin does, "My body is a fundamentally inner body; the body of the other is a fundamentally outer body" (*Estetika* 44). The point is that my exposedness makes me other. As the one-in-responsibility, my body is drawn and laid down, broken to be offered up for the other: the last act is the Eucharist. As the one strikes up against the other in the dialogical relation, the other cuts into the one to the point at which subjectivity becomes a matter of being "accused of what the others do or suffer, or responsible for what they do or suffer," in the words of Levinas. "The uniqueness of the self is the very fact of bearing the fault of another" (*Otherwise* 112). Reading these lines, one cannot help but recall Bakhtin's thoughts on Christ in *Aesthetics of Verbal Art*, where he writes, "Christ opposes *I* and the *other:* absolute sacrifice for himself, absolute charity for the other" (*Estetika* 52). It is not the empathetic union of I and the other that characterizes responsibility but the absolute difference that summons the charity of nonindifference. We should understand Bakhtin in the light of this idea when he writes, "Living through the sufferings of another, I experience them precisely as *his* sufferings, in the category of *other*, and my reaction to him is not a cry of pain but a word of comfort and a helping hand" (*Estetika* 25-26). While pain differs one from another, it also refers one to another. I live through the sufferings of another by bearing responsibility for the other; I become responsible for the other—and thus bear witness to the summons—by offering a helping hand. Taking the other's part, again, does not entail losing myself in the other but taking his suffering and his fault upon myself. In this way I become a self.

Responsibility, then, is subjectivity, and subjectivity means substitution, as Levinas describes it: "Constituting itself in the very movement wherein being responsible for the other devolves on it, subjectivity goes to the point of substitution for the Other. It assumes the condition—or the uncondition—of hostage. Subjectivity as such is initially hostage; it answers to the point of expiating for others" (*Ethics* 100). Uncondition, thrown out of context, hanging by the heels, staring into the abyss—such is subjectivity. It is the place where Eden and Gethsemane intersect, both fallen and redeeming. The sense in which *hostage* must be taken is as a cognate not of the Latin *hostis* but of *hostia,* host, the eucharistic bread: this is my body, take it, I put it in your place. The "formula" is not "I suffer, therefore I am" but "I suffer, therefore you are."

In *Otherwise than Being*, we find an elaboration of this point: "To undergo outrage from the other is an absolute patience only if by this from-the-other is already for-the-other. This transfer . . . is subjectivity itself. 'To tend the other cheek to the smiter and be filled with shame' [Lamentations 3:30] . . . is not to draw from suffering some kind of redemptive virtue. In the trauma of persecution it is to pass from the outrage undergone to the responsibility for the persecutor, and, in this sense from suffering to expiation for the other" (111). The transfer from from-the-other to for-the-other is the transfer from suffering to expiation. This interchange is not only subjectivity, as Levinas says, but the interaction of dialogical relation. One cannot engage in dialogue without being smitten. One cannot live without offering up one's life in expiation for the other and thereby finding expiation for oneself. In the realm of human being, signification is expiation. Or, as Levinas states it, "in its *being* subjectivity undoes *essence* by substituting itself for another. Qua one-for-another, it is absorbed in signification, in saying or the verb form of the infinite. Signification precedes essence" (*Otherwise* 13). There can be no expiation without this undoing of essence.

Here lies an important implication of the dialogical relation. To transfer the word from my mouth to the mouth of the other is to receive the word and deed of the other; it is to become responsible, as the parent is responsible for the vulgar word that comes from the mouth of the child. The self is this locus of transfer that defines responsibility within the dialogical relation, always rushing ahead of itself to answer for what has been. Dasein's past, in the words of Heidegger, "does not follow after but already goes ahead" (*Sein* 20). This may shed some light on a cryptic remark made by Bakhtin: "For me, memory is memory of the future; for the other, it is memory of the past" (*Estetika* 110). Memory of the future is my mindfulness of the response and expiation I have yet to make in view of what the other has suffered, uttered, or done. It is the vision of the future perfect of what I shall have been for what I am in the process of becoming. The passage from past to future in this instance is the passage from suffering to expiation, from outrage to responsibility. And we are forever in passage. Once again we hear Levinas reminding us that "in front of the face, I always demand more of myself; the more I respond to it, the more the demand grows" ("Signature" 186). In the instant it takes to respond, I am an instant behind in my response. I have allowed something to slip by, and I cannot slip away. What remains, what beckons me from the face, is the trace of what precedes all beginnings. This anarchic trace, as Levinas terms it, is the "excluded middle" (*Otherwise* 97) upon which turns my memory of the future and the other's memory of the past. It is the thing that "commands in the face of the other" (*Otherwise* 97) and thus calls me to expiation for the other.

On Bakhtin's view, however, there is one in whom the alpha and omega of the one-for-the-other are gathered, the Trace Himself, as it were; he is the one who has drained the cup, allowing nothing to slip by: "In Christ we find, in all its depth, the single synthesis of *ethical solipsism*, of infinite severity of man toward himself—that is, an irreproachably pure relation to himself—with the *ethical-aesthetic goodness* toward the other: here for the first time appears an infinitely profound *I-for-myself*, . . . immeasurably good to the other, rendering the whole truth to the other as such, revealing and confirming in all its fullness the precious originality of the other" (*Estetika* 51). And recall: "Christ opposes *I* and the *other*: absolute sacrifice for himself, absolute charity for the other. . . . That which I must be for the other is what God is for me" (*Estetika* 52). Bakhtin here brings out the all-or-nothing of responsibility. God's other is man. God's infinity is His infinite severity toward Himself—the offering up of His Son—for the sake of His other. His divinity lies in the renunciation of His godhead, in turning Himself into love by transforming suffering into expiation, outrage into responsibility. What God is for me, I must be for the other, transforming from-the-other into for-the-other, not in a usurpation of God but in an effacement of myself in the face of the other. Along these lines Clark and Holquist explain, "Bakhtin's insistence on the necessity of 'understanding' the position not only of the other but of all others, by adding communication theory to theology, extends the meaning of Christ's biblical injunction to treat others as we would be treated ourselves, to take on, in other words, the role of others with the same depth of sympathy and understanding that we bring to our own perception of ourselves. In Bakhtin's system this is not merely a normal imperative but an epistemological requirement" (208). Such is the absolute opposition of I and other, the *dia*logic of the dialogical relation.

In Bakhtin's statement concerning Christ, however, we immediately notice a contrast with Levinas's terminology. Where Bakhtin says "I-for-myself" Levinas speaks of "the other in the same." Yet the difference is only a difference in terms, not in sense. Both are determinative of subjectivity as responsibility, as the process not of giving signs but of giving oneself as a sign. It is the other's disturbance of me and within me that leads me to signify myself. Arguing that "the *other* is first of all *I-for-myself*" (*Estetika* 52), Bakhtin thus believes that for-the-other and for-oneself are of a piece; as he sees it, the other in the same is also the same in the other. "What is *mine*," he insists, "is not in me and for me but in the other" (*Estetika* 101). Like the God who is manifest in the Christ and there takes on the sins of the other, I am called to an absolute responsibility for the other—to the point of substitution, of the same in the other—and that is how I forge a self for myself. Just as God renounces Himself to become love, so must I renounce myself to become love, that is, to become a self in the affirmation of "the precious originality of the other." In this affirmation, in this response, absolute difference, again, becomes absolute nonindifference, which is expiation both for the self and for the other. The movement of expiation, then, is the highest affirmation of the dearness of the other and of life, and such affirmation is precisely the point of dialogical relation. The expiation I offer is my testament; the responsibility I meet is my testimony.

But to whom, it must be asked, do I testify? Lacan offers one reply when he says, "Who, then, is this other to whom I am more attached than to myself, since, at the heart of my assent to my own identity it is still he who agitates me? . . . This other is the Other that even my lie invokes as a guarantor of the truth in which it subsists. By which we can also see that it is with the appearance of language that the dimension of truth emerges" (*Écrits* 172). Levinas hints at a similar response to this question by explaining that responsibility "is troubled and becomes a problem when a third party enters. . . . The other stands in a relationship with a third party"(*Otherwise* 157). I come before the other, but the relation *between* the other and me comes under the eye of a third, which, in Lacan's words, "imposes itself as a witness to the Truth" (*Écrits* 305); one word for the thing that disturbs me is *truth*. Levinas suggests further that the third party is another neighbor who witnesses the relation between oneself and the other (*Otherwise* 157); the I-Thou relation always exists within a community. While this is indeed the case, it is only part of the larger picture, for the Third abides whether another neighbor is there or not. To be sure, Levinas implies this when he says, "The representation of signification is itself born in the signifyingness of proximity in the measure that a third party is alongside the neighbor" (*Otherwise* 83). This third party is the source of the disturbance of the other in the same: the thing that stirs and inspires me issues from the other and from beyond him.

Bakhtin demonstrates his sense for the presence of the Third when he states, "Every dialogue proceeds as though against the background of a responsive understanding of a Third who is invisibly present, standing above all the participants in the dialogue" (*Estetika* 306). It is the dialogical relation that posits the relation to the Third; and the Third posits the responsibility, not the other way around. Levinas brings this out by saying, "The Infinite always remains 'third person'—'He' in spite of the 'You' ('Thou,' 'Tu') whose face concerns me. The Infinite affects the I without the I's being able to dominate it, without the I's being able to 'assume' through the *arche* of the Logos the unboundedness of the Infinite thus *anarchically* affecting the I, imprinting itself as a trace in the absolute passivity—prior to all freedom—showing itself as a 'Responsibility-for-the-Other' which this affection gives rise to" ("Signature" 188-89). Both for Levinas and for Bakhtin, the Third represents a realm of truth that decides the significance of any relation between the one and the other. Without this other relation, in which *within* and *above* are synonyms, there can be no meaning or significance, no signification or responsibility. Bakhtin is quite explicit on this point, describing the Third in his "Notes from 1970-1971" as "the overman, the over-*I*—that is, the witness and judge of every man (of every *I*)" (*Estetika* 342). Levinas also uses judicial language in this regard, asserting that "justice is this very presence of the third party and this manifestation, for which every secret, every intimacy is a dissimulation" (*Otherwise* 191). Dissimulation here is precisely what lies outside—or flees from— dialogical relation. The one to whom we bear witness and by whom we are inspired or in-spirited, on the other hand, stands apart from yet is included in the dialogical relation. It is the thing by which the breath—the *pneuma*—of responsibility is drawn and through which the self is made into an offering, and not a fugitive.

SPIRIT: THE OFFERING OF THE SELF

Let us begin our discussion of the spirit with a comparison of the distinctions between soul and spirit made by Bakhtin and Levinas. In Bakhtin's *Aesthetics of Verbal Art*, for example, we read, "I experience the internal life of the other as soul; within myself I live in spirit. The soul is an image of the totality of all that is truly experienced, of all that is at hand, in the soul in time; the spirit, however, is the totality of all meaningful significance and direction in life, of all the acts issuing from itself" (*Estetika* 97-98). Rather than use the word *experience* in this case, perhaps it would be better to say my *relation* to the other is a relation to a soul as an individual instance of a universal being. Encountering the other, I have a soul placed in my charge: I am *charged* with the other, in every sense of the term, because the other is soul. And I am so charged to the extent that I have a soul, not as a possession but as an offering. Says Bakhtin, "The soul (both mine and the other's) cannot be given as a thing (the appropriate object of natural sciences) but only in the signifying expression or realization in texts, both for itself and for the other" (*Estetika* 284). In these lines we find an expression of the definitive link between the soul and the one-for-the-other of signification. To say that within myself I live in spirit, moreover, is to declare my responsibility *before* the other *to* the Third. My meaning rests on my relation to the totality of meaning, which is spirit. And the portal to the relation to the totality is the relation to the other.

Levinas addresses this matter when he writes, "The soul would live only for the disclosure of being which arouses it or provokes it; it would be a moment of the life of the Spirit, that is, of Being-totality, leaving nothing outside of itself, the same finding again the same" (*Otherwise* 28). Recalling here Levinas's statement that "subjectivity is the restlessness of the same disturbed by the other" (*Otherwise* 25), we realize that the soul lives by the storm and dizziness of this disturbance; it lives as it is provoked. Characterized by a longing to be an individual expression of the totality, the soul finds through its relation to the other the desired relation to the spirit. Nothing is outside of itself, so that it is responsible to the spirit for all.

Both Bakhtin and Levinas, then, associate the spirit with a totality and the soul with an expression of that totality; spirit and soul are related as truth and giving voice to truth are related. The soul becomes a moment in the life of the spirit through a signification that bears witness to the truth of all meaningful significance, the truth that makes meaning an issue. The soul is the event that occurs when, in answering for the other, I answer to the spirit. In living for the disclosure of the spirit, the soul lives in the exposure of itself, in the vulnerability of responsibility, as "an exposedness always to be exposed the more," to borrow from Levinas; "an exposure to expressing, and thus to saying, thus to giving" (*Otherwise* 50). Spirit is always born from a wound, the wound through which the other enters the same in an act of response. The summons to speak is a summons to break and bleed: the only thing that is truly mine to give is my truth and testimony, my body and blood. Therein lies my soul. A human being has no soul apart from a relation to spirit or to truth; a human being has no relation to the spirit apart from signification and responsibility, that is, apart from an offering of the self. Whatever soul or substance I have always arises from the ashes of this offering. As I rise, I have more to offer, so that the offering is never complete. Bakhtin brings out an implication of the point that the offering always falls short when he asserts, "The soul is spirit unrealized for itself, reflected in the loving consciousness of another (person, God)" (*Estetika* 98). The spirit is the loving consciousness that abides not within the one but *between* the one and the other; the thing reflected is the soul offered to the other and received by the one. Bakhtin uses the word "person" as we have used the word "other," and what he regards as God we here regard as spirit, what Levinas refers to as "the glory of the Infinite" or "the glory of God." The loving consciousness, moreover, is expressed in the offering of the self. To love the other is to offer oneself, making oneself into a sign, one-for-the-other. Only in this way do we receive the sign.

Proximity, then, is more spiritual than spatial. It has more to do with signification than with situation and lies in a responsibility that is the opposite of repose. Viewed as spirit unrealized for itself, the soul is in a constant state of unrest, continually summoned by the spirit to make the needful offering. There is no place to hide. Those who seek the cover of darkness are seized all the more by the light; the more we would place our hands over our ears, the louder the call. Such is the unimpeachable assignation that, like a thorn in the flesh, allows us no sleep. Says Levinas, "A fraternity that cannot be abrogated, an unimpeachable assignation, proximity is an impossibility to move away without the torsion of a complex, without 'alienation' or fault. This insomnia is the psyche" (*Otherwise* 87).

In Emerson's explanation of Bakhtin's notion of the psyche, we can see that it is close to Levinas's: "In the Bakhtinian model, every individual engages in two perpendicular activities. He forms lateral ('horizontal') relationships with other individuals in specific speech acts, and he simultaneously forms internal ('vertical') relationships between the outer world and his own psyche. The double activities are constant, and their interactions in fact *constitute* the psyche. The psyche is thus not an internal but a boundary phenomenon" ("Outer" 249). There is no being *there* without being *with*. But this being with is not simply tarrying alongside; in the words of Heidegger, "Dasein, as being-with, comes to being-for-the-other" (*Sein* 123). Conversely, being *for* is what establishes our being *with*. This is what lies behind Levinas's use of the word *fraternity* above: I live in brotherhood *with*, not merely in the company *of*, others. Levinas's phrase "the torsion of a complex" is also well chosen. The breakdown of the dialogical relation is a twisting of the word and of the self whose language is the word. The torsion is the symptom Lacan speaks of when he says, "The symptom resolves itself entirely in a Language analysis, because the symptom itself is structured like a language, because the symptom is a Language from which the Word must be delivered" (*Language* 32). And the word is delivered in the offering of the self, by which it becomes spirit.

The insomnia of the soul in proximity thus underscores its relation to spirit and constitutes what Bakhtin calls "a special responsibility" (*Estetika* 179). Recall here Levinas's remark that "in the form of responsibility, the psyche in the soul is the other in me, a malady of identity, both accused and *self*, the same for the other, the same by the other" (*Otherwise* 69). Responsibility is the wakefulness sustained by the call; once heard, it is always heard.

The insomnia of the soul points up its constantly hearing a summons it cannot refuse and a question to which it must forever respond: Where are you? As the spirit's disturbance of the soul, this unrest is prior to any questions concerning freedom. As Levinas has observed, "the Good is not presented to freedom; it has chosen me before I have chosen it" (*Otherwise* 11). Freedom comes with responsibility, not the other way around; becoming answerable to "the Good," the individual becomes free. The assignation, the call, is antecedent to the issues that create the contexts for freedom. Lacan has argued that "it is the world of words which creates the world of things" (*Language* 39), and in Heidegger's *On the Way to Language* we read, "Where the word fails, there is no thing" (*Unterwegs* 163). Freely translated, these statements tell us that first the self offers itself, answering before it is called, and then the contextual questions that constitute the world arise. Hence, in the words of Bakhtin, "the spirit cannot be a carrier of a theme" (*Estetika* 98). Instead, the spirit is the carrier of the carrier, the source of every sign and all signification. It is what Bakhtin describes when he writes, "The inner infinity bursts forth and finds no rest: the principle of life" (*Estetika* 179). Once again the insomnia of the soul comes to mind. The infinite bursts forth in the offering of the self to and for the other. It does not cause the offering—it *is* the offering, in the wake of which the waters of the self are once again disturbed.

Thus in the relation to the spirit, response is a hearing. We remember Heidegger's words: "Man speaks in that he responds to language. This responding is a hearing. It hears because it listens to the command of stillness" (*Poetry* 210). Heidegger's "command" is much like Levinas's "assignation." And what Heidegger here regards as language is the dwelling place of spirit, of the Other Lacan invokes when he asserts, "It is from the Other that the subject receives even the message that he emits" (*Écrits* 305). The word's *is* is prior to every *was* ("Before Abraham was," says the word, "I am"); this is a notion that lies behind Levinas's declaration that "the saying that comes to me is my own word" (*Otherwise* 150). To say "Here I am" is to say "I hear." As Levinas puts it in *Ethics and Infinity,* "When in the presence of the Other I say 'Here I am!' this 'Here I am!' is the place through which the Infinite enters into language, but without giving itself to be seen" (106). He goes on to explain, "The witness testifies to what was said by himself. For he has said 'Here I am!' before the Other; and from the fact that before the Other he recognizes the responsibility which is incumbent upon himself, he has manifested what the face of the Other signified for him. The glory of the Infinite reveals itself through what it is capable of doing in the witness" (109). When once told that atheists everywhere were demanding proofs of God's existence, the Hasidic Rebbe Pinhas of Koretz is said to have seized the sacred scrolls from the Holy Ark and shouted, "I *swear* that God exists! What more proof can there be?" Laying his hands on the Word, he declares "Here I am!" before the Other. The spirit enters through the portal of this "Here I am!" both carried upon and carrying the passion: the offering and the outcry are themselves the Holy Ark. "Man passionately longs to hear the voice of God," Berdyaev has said, "but he can hear it only in and through himself" (*Destiny* 53–54).

We think we pray to God, but such is not exactly the case, for the prayer itself is divinity. "In saying itself," Heidegger has written, "the nearness of God is given" (*Unterwegs* 219). When we look upon the world and see God, it is God who sees through our eyes. The spirit or the glory of the Infinite is at once subject and object, or rather it is all subject, the constitutive feature of a subjectivity defined by the offering of itself. Levinas's assertion that "subjectivity is the other in the same" (*Otherwise*) once more comes to mind; and recall again Bakhtin's statement that "what is *mine* is not in me and for me but in the other" (*Estetika* 101). It is the presence of the Third, of spirit, that creates this transformation of difference into nonindifference, of imposition into assignation. When my responsibility goes to the point of being responsible for the fault of the other—when I tend the other cheek to the smiter— the spirit speaks in the saying of that rsponsibility. For this saying, despite me and for the other, is the affirmation of the spirit issuing from the one offered to the other. "In proximity, in signification, in my giving of signs," Levinas declares, "already the Infinite speaks through the witness I bear of it, in my sincerity, in my saying without said, preoriginary saying which is said in the mouth of the very one that receives the witness" (*Otherwise* 151). Again, in my response I answer before I am called, called in my answering. As the spirit speaks in my response, I am beckoned all the more to respond. The more is always there; the inner infinity continually bursts forth, becoming an exteriority that again turns into an inwardness, turning the inside out.

Here Levinas helps us to see a connection between spirit and inwardness: "Inwardness is not a secret place somewhere in me; it is that reverting in which the eminently exterior, precisely in virtue of this eminent exteriority, this impossibility of being contained and consequently entering into a theme, forms, as infinity, an exception to essence, concerns me and circumscribes me and orders me by my own voice. The command is stated by the mouth of him it commands. The infinitely exterior becomes an 'inward' voice, but a voice bearing witness to the fission of the inward secrecy that makes signs to another, signs of this very giving of signs" (*Otherwise* 147). Levinas evokes a wholeness reminiscent of the unity Bakhtin speaks of when he says, "*A unity is not the unity of the object or of the event but the unity of an embrace, of an inclusion of the object and the event*" (*Esthétique* 76). Here—where subjectivity is the other in the same, where responsibility *to* is responsibility *for*, where the self receives itself in the offering of itself—here the relation to spirit is at once all-exclusive and all-inclusive. The particular loses its importance, yet it is included in the manifestation of the most needful and the most high. When the spirit speaks through its witness, it reveals itself to its witness through the other: wholly Other, the spirit is wholly same, the same who finds itself in the same. Truth or spirit is dialogical because, in manifesting itself to itself, spirit tears away from itself and returns to itself. In the words of Levinas, "this way in which the Other or the Infinite manifests itself in subjectivity is the very phenomenon of 'inspiration,' and consequently defines the psychic element, the very pneumatic of the psychism" (*Ethics* 108). Whoever goes forth to the other in an offering of the self bears what cannot be contained and finds what cannot be sought: the sign of this very giving of signs, the sign of spirit.

The call comes from me and from beyond me. The penetration of the limits of possibility is a penetration inward, to the place of the voice for which speaking and hearing are of a piece. Deep calls to deep, and from the depths the offering is made. Spirit means the union of absolute exclusiveness and absolute inclusiveness. Face-to-face with the other, I do not ignore everything else but behold everything else, the world itself, in the face of the other. Hence the Talmudic saying: To save a single life is to save the whole world. And to be responsible for a single human being is to be responsible for all before all. Indeed, Levinas cites a statement from Dostoevsky's *The Brothers Karamazov* along these lines: "I am I in the sole measure that I am responsible, a non-interchangeable I. I can substitute myself for everyone, but no one can substitute himself for me. Such is my inalienable identity of subject. It is in this precise sense that Dostoevsky said: '*We are all responsible for all, for all men before all, and I more than all the others*' (*Ethics* 101). Thus when we hear Bakhtin declare, "The soul is the gift of my spirit to the *other*" (*Estetika* 116), we may understand him to mean that the soul is an offering of the noninterchangeable I, of the totality of self, to the other for the sake of all. The offering of the self is an opening of the Infinite, a murmuring of the spirit.

Face-to-face with the other, then, we encounter in the face something beyond the limits of representation. In the words of Levinas, "the face of the other in proximity, which is more than representation, is an unrepresentable trace, the way of the Infinite" (*Otherwise* 116). Proximity is the place of the spirit, the *between* etched by the trace; the spirit is known by its tracks. In proximity, what is farthest is nearest. And the notion that the other contains the all in a union of exclusiveness and inclusiveness Levinas expresses by saying, "Being takes on signification and becomes a universe . . . because in an approach, there is inscribed or written the trace of infinity, the trace of a departure, but trace of what is inordinate, does not enter into the present, and inverts the *arche* into anarchy, that there is forsakenness of the other, obsession by him, responsibility and a self" (*Otherwise* 117). With the inversion of the beginning into something that "precedes" the beginning, obsession by the other becomes offering to the other, and forsakenness of the other becomes offering for the other. The trace of a departure summons the departure from the self, the tearing of the self from itself, and is therefore the trace of the self as spirit. The becoming that characterizes the spiritual life of the self is the becoming of a universe; signification happens, and the life and the world in which I encounter the other *matter*. Finitude is no longer a euphemism for nothingness but a vessel of the infinite, of what cannot be contained.

What Levinas refers to as the trace of infinity we may understand as the spirit. It is by virtue of the spirit that being takes on
signification and that signification takes place; and signification
can take place only in responsibility. The spirit breathes life into
the word, which constitutes the dialogical relation that summons
the offering of the self. That the trace is inscribed or written points
up its contact with the word. Indeed, the trace is precisely the
word as spirit, the word that gives significance to words and
eloquence to silence. It is what Bakhtin deems the "still *latent,
unuttered future Word*" (*Problems* 90), posterior to all endings and
anterior to all beginnings. Bakhtin's unuttered future is Levinas's
inverted *arche*, and both proclaim an eternity into which the posterior and anterior are gathered. We need not fly to the mountain
tops of Tibet or to desert places in order to behold the spirit. It is
here before us, calling out from the careworn lines in the face of an
old man, from the frightened look in the eyes of a child.

In "Signature" Levinas writes, "Illumination and sense dawn
only with the existing beings' rising up and establishing themselves in this horrible neutrality of the *there is*" (181). He comments
further on the rumbling emptiness that he calls the "there is" in
Ethics and Infinity: "It is a noise returning after every negation of this
noise. Neither nothingness nor being. . . . One cannot say of this
'there is' which persists that it is nothingness, even though there is
nothing. *Existence and Existents* tries to describe this horrible thing,
and moreover describes it as horror and panic" (48-49). Nonindifference before the face becomes an issue in the face of the
profound indifference of the "there is." Rather like the stone wall of
Dostoevsky's underground man, the " 'there is,' " Levinas explains, "is the phenomenon of impersonal being: 'it' " (*Ethics* 48).
If subjectivity is tied to responsibility, it is also linked to the silence
that the subject encounters—or collides with—in the midst of the
"there is." The task that confronts the human being is to generate
a responsive voice that will not be drowned by the droning silence
of the "there is," a voice that will live in the silent eloquence of the
"Thou art."

The foregoing effort to connect signification, responsibility, and
spirit through a comparison of Bakhtin and Levinas has been
made against the background of the "there is." It stands over
against the impersonal It-world of the ready-made, what Bakhtin

associates with official monologism when he asserts, "The dialogic means of seeking the truth is counterposed to *official* monologism, which pretends to *possess a ready-made truth*" (*Problems* 110). Seeking truth: that is what signification, responsibility, and spirit are about. While Bakhtin and Levinas may have some differences in their terms and even in their positions, they are at one in their counterposition. The light that Bakhtin attempts to shed on the truth burns in the shadow of Stalin, and Levinas's words are replete with the silence of six million victims of the It-world. As we draw the two thinkers into a dialogue and engage in a dialogue with them, our responsibility announces itself: we are commanded by our own mouths. Any truth that we turn up lies not in what we discover but in what we offer, not in our understanding but in our ability to respond, "Here I am." Thus we leave the confines of this essay to come once again before the countenance, knowing, in the words of T.S. Eliot, that there is "No place of grace for those who avoid the face / No time to rejoice for those who walk among noise and deny the voice" (64).

But where, we ask, is the place of grace? This is the question that takes us or calls us to the fifth and final essay in this volume. Our concern all along has been with literature and spirit; it is time to situate both the concern and its topic. Moving onward, we are reminded that at every turn the "hero" or topic of this work has emerged neither in Bakhtin nor in another figure but *between* the two: this space between has been the chronotope of our investigation. Clark and Holquist, in fact, have noted that Bakhtin's own accent is on "the *Zwischenwelt,* or the world between consciousness" (9). Now that space itself will be our focus. And, with the help of Bakhtin and Heidegger, we shall find that in this space is the place of grace, the *templum* of word and being, and the site of literature and spirit.

FIVE

Bakhtin and Heidegger

Word and Being

Mikhail Bakhtin and Martin Heidegger are two of the twentieth century's most profound thinkers in the philosophy of language, particularly with respect to the ontology of language, or the relation between word and being. Both, moreover, turn to literature in the development of their thinking on language—Bakhtin to Rabelais and Dostoevsky, for example, and Heidegger to poets such as Hölderlin, Rilke, and Trakl. In his pursuit of the word, Heidegger became famous for his statement that "language is the house of being" in "What Are Poets For?" (*Poetry* 132; also *Unterwegs* 254). And in *Problems of Dostoevsky's Poetics*, Bakhtin argues that "an overwhelming part of reality is contained in the form of a still *latent, unuttered future Word*" (90). In these statements alone we see not only a link between word and being but the problem of locating both. Much more than Heidegger, however, Bakhtin emphasizes the importance of the interaction between speaker and listener in his approach to the word, or discourse. It will also be noted that Bakhtin places, perhaps, a stronger accent on the religious dimensions of his philosophy of language. Indeed, Clark and Holquist have noted this: "Bakhtin sought God not in what John of the Cross called 'the flight of the alone to the alone' but in the exact opposite, the space between men that can be bridged by the word, by utterance. Instead of seeking God's place in stasis and silence, Bakhtin sought it in energy and communication. In seeking a connection between God and men, Bakhtin concentrated on the forces enabling connections, in society and in language, between men" (62). Bakhtin's concern, in short, lies with the event of the word—both uttered and unuttered—while Heidegger's thinking generally addresses the metaphysics of language and the notion of being.

Both thinkers, nevertheless, subscribe to the idea that any sense of being or reality we may generate issues not from observation but from articulation. "The event of being," as Clark and Holquist describe Bakhtin's position, "is specified as an act of communication" (206); with some explanation, this statement applies to Heidegger as well. Clark and Holquist, in fact, point out an important corollary to this view, as well as a similarity between Bakhtin and Heidegger, with respect to the bridging between mind and world: "The term Bakhtin proposes for this bridging function is 'answerability' (close to Heidegger's *Sorge*, a response to the 'call' or *Ruf* of Being), where the responding aspect of the word, the *otvet* of *otvetstvennost'*, is given its fullest weight. Responsibility is conceived as the action of responding to the world's need, and is accomplished through the activity of the self's responding to its own need for an other" (77). The other is essential to the establishment of a between space where the bridging takes place. As we have seen in the preceding essays, the *between happens* with the appearance of the other. In the ensuing comparison of Bakhtin and Heidegger it will be shown that word and being reside neither "in here" nor "out there," neither in the mouth of the speaker nor in the mind of the listener, but in between. To create this "between" is to create a place for human being, and it is the fundamental task that confronts every living I who stands before a living Thou. Let us consider, then, what underlies the task, what it entails, and what is at stake.

THE WORD AND THE BETWEEN

Where does the word come from? It emerges from the between, from what Heidegger calls *das Zwischen* when, in *Being and Time*, he says, "As care, Dasein *is* 'the Between' " (*Sein* 374). It comes not as a sound but as a summons to the answerability that is care or nonindifference. The word reaches out, calls out, for the human being to pour himself out into the between. The between, then, is the place or the vessel into which the word is poured, and with the word the self, as the word becomes flesh. This pouring out is the emerging from. The between, in turn, arises from the word; one goes with the other, just as the mountain goes with the valley. Says Voloshinov in *Marxism and the Philosophy of Language,* the word "is precisely a *product* of the *interrelation between speaker and listener*" (*Marksizm* 87)—not a product of speaker and listener, be it noted, but of the interrelation *between.* The between, indeed, is not so much a place as an event, the event of interrelation into which the place, the *where,* of speaker and listener is gathered. The two stand at the poles, and they are indeed indispensable to the event of the word as it emerges from the between and the between emerges from it. But the word itself rises up in the polarity, in the passion, between an I and a Thou. Heidegger claims that the passion from which the word is born is gratitude, which he defines in *Signposts* as "the echo of the kindness of Being" (*Wegmarken* 105). The thanksgiving that forms the wellspring of the word, however, is gratitude not only for blessing but for trial, if it is in truth an echo of being. And trial occurs wherever there is an encounter with what is alien, or other. The other is the one who brings us to the edge and situates us at the pole, drawing us into the tension between the poles. The other is the one who penetrates me to cut a wound into me, myself between myself.

It is in this connection that we hear Bakhtin declare, "The word is shaped in dialogic encounter with an alien word" (*Dialogic* 279). And: "Discourse lives, as it were, on the boundary between its own context and another, alien context. . . . Dialogic interaction becomes, as it were, an event of discourse itself" (*Dialogic* 284). The between is the place and polarity of dialogue, and its substance— the stuff of the between—is discourse. Wherever the between arises in the dialogical interaction of I and Thou, discourse is the subject of discourse, as well as its issue. Word begets word, just as author begets hero, Thou begets I. As Heidegger expresses it in *Elucidations of Hölderlin's Poetry,* "we—human beings—are a dialogue. The being of man is grounded in language, but this genuinely happens only in dialogue" (*Erläuterungen* 36). Saying Thou, I become I; offering the word, I receive the word from out of the between. Like the I, the word answers before it is called and summons in its response: it lives *in the midst.* When two come together dialogically, the edge or boundary is precisely the middle, at once as thin as the line between a man and his shadow and as boundless as the abyss. To move in the midst is to come to the threshold. The word is an event that occurs at the threshold of relation; the word is forever at the threshold, not what is uttered but what is about to be uttered, a saying that pulsates between *was* and *yet-to-be*. Conceived as discourse (a concept included in the Russian *slovo*), the word is a portal through which we pass to encounter the other and ourselves in a space between both.

In this regard Heidegger notes, "In accordance with its spatiality, Dasein is never in the first instance here but is rather there, from out of which it returns to its Here" (*Sein* 107-8). In accordance with my spatiality, I incorporate what is outside of me into the landscape of my inner life: it is in the light of the between that I have an inner life. Recall once more Bakhtin's remark: "My body is fundamentally an inner body; the body of the other is fundamentally an outer body" (*Estetika* 44). This statement is something of a definition of the between, as is Bakhtin's claim that "I myself am entirely *within* my life, and if I myself should somehow see the *outwardness* of my life, then this seen outwardness would immediately become a feature of the inwardness (as experienced) of my life" (*Estetika* 76-77). The *here* and *there* Heidegger refers to, then, must be understood in terms of the between; Dasein—being there—means being between, and being between means moving inward or hither. Each I, every Thou, arrives at his here by means of a discourse that is between; the between is the realm of discourse. Foucault, it will be recalled, makes a similar point when he insists, "Discourse is not the majestically unfolding manifestation of a thinking, knowing, speaking subject, but, on the contrary, a totality, in which the dispersion of the subject and his discontinuity with himself may be determined. It is a space of exteriority in which a network of distinct sites is deployed" (*Archaeology* 55). The movement from between to here is what Heidegger has in mind when he says, "We not only speak *the* language, we speak *out of it*" (*Unterwegs* 254)—out of the language and into ourselves: my inward life is my life within the word. And we are able to speak out of language because we are discontinuous; what we are is never settled, and something of what we have to say is always yet to be said, calling from the between and awaiting our response.

One way of thinking about the relation of the word to the between is to say that the tie that binds them is the yet-to-be. The between is at once spatial and temporal, is chronotopic; or rather, the between *is* the chronotope. It is not, of course, the space-time of the physicist but a space-time characterized by the inversions of there into here and the intersection of the future perfect with the present tense. "Surpassing is there," as Heidegger states it in his own terms, "in the fact of being-there (Dasein)" (*Essence* 39). If, moreover, one's genuine life is lived in the word, then the word is most genuine when "populated with one's own intention," as Bakhtin puts it (*Dialogic* 293). And if we concede a kinship between intention and resolve, then the sort of temporality that links the word and the between comes out in the following statement by Heidegger: "It remains a distinction of the temporality of authentic existence that, in resolve, it never loses time and 'always has time.' For its present, the temporality of resolve, has the character of the *instant*. The instant's authentic way of making the situation present does not lead itself on but is rather *sustained* in the future of what shall have been" (*Sein* 410). To state it differently, viewed in terms of the resolve that authenticates the word, the instant is not the *now* of the here but the *yet-to-be* of the between, which is revealed in the word. Resolve brings the individual to the threshold of the instant. "Forming itself in an atmosphere of the already spoken," Bakhtin writes, "the word is at the same time determined by that which has not been said but which is needed" (*Dialogic* 280). Heidegger states the relation of the temporality of the said to the temporality of the needed by saying, "Only insofar as Dasein generally *is* as having-*been* can it have yet to come to itself, can it *return* (Sein 325-26). And the temporality of what is needed—the temporality of return—is the temporality of resolve. It is the call of the needful that summons the word from the between, a call that comes *not yet*, and so resolve declares, "Before you call, I shall answer."

This brings us to an important relation between silence and the word, for it is in silence that what is needful calls out. Silence is the vessel of the yet-to-be, forever haunted by the word on the threshold of utterance. The openness opened up by the word is the open-endedness of silence. The notion of prayer may shed some light on this point. Prayer is the language of silence and the substance of language. When we give voice to the word with our whole being, when we are one with our address to the Thou and with our silence toward the Thou, our utterance bears the features of prayer. In the silence of prayer we live in relation to the word, to the eternal Thou, to the call of being. In the silence of prayer we encounter the silence of the between, where the word dwells as "that which has not been said but which is needed," as that which constitutes the call of being. To be sure, Heidegger has asserted that "the call speaks in the uncanny mode of *silence*" (*Sein* 277). The utterance of the Nameless is heard as what cannot be uttered, as what speaks and listens at the same time, silently. This silent summons of being is what vibrates in the polarity of the yet-to-be between speaker and listener. The word, moreover, is born from that polarity *between* not only as summons but as response. Hence we find Heidegger declaring, "Man speaks insofar as he responds to language. This responding is a hearing. It hears insofar as it listens to the command of silence" (*Unterwegs* 32-33). Again, before you call, I shall answer, and in answering I shall hear the call.

Bakhtin adds to the light Heidegger sheds by pointing out that every utterance of discourse is an active response and not an isolated assertion. "The perception and understanding of the meaning of speech," he writes in "The Problem of Verbal Genres," "simultaneously assume an active, responsive position in relation to speech (fully or partially), filling it out. . . . Every understanding of living speech, of living expression, bears an actively responsive character" (*Estetika* 246). Further, "every speaker is himself a respondent. For he is not the first to speak, not the first to breach the eternal silence of the universe" (*Estetika* 247). Nothing is lost. The words we utter abide, making us into respondents, making us capable of response and therefore response-able. The word and the between are linked through responsibility. To be a respondent is to be responsible; to be a respondent is to live in the tension of inner and outer that distinguish the between. Responsibility, moreover, is an active condition, so that the between is never fixed or static but is forever in flux. The "understanding" Bakhtin refers to, then, is not simply an acknowledgment or a deciphering of a statement but is an answering to and answering for the word. I cannot understand without becoming responsible; the message that comes forth from the between transforms me into a messenger and a witness.

Coupling Bakhtin with Heidegger, we see more clearly that the word is the means by which we not only speak but also hear and understand. Language speaks, Heidegger tells us, "only insofar as it summons the one called to come . . . into the between of the difference" (*Unterwegs* 28). And the one called is summoned by his own responsive word; as Levinas expresses it, "the saying that comes to me is my own word" (*Otherwise* 150). To say "I am commanded" is to say "I understand." Once again, one does not imply two, but two are needed to posit one. Recall here Bakhtin's remark that "in *understanding* there are two consciousnesses, two subjects" (*Estetika* 289). This statement adds helpful perspective to Heidegger's assertion that "listening is the existential being-open of Dasein as being-with, for the other" (*Sein* 163). Thus understanding is a response that makes difference into the nonindifference of responsibility; the between is made of responsibility. Because speaking and hearing are both responsive, they do not take place strictly at the poles of listener and speaker but occur in the between, in the event of dialogical interaction; in that *interaction* the two at the poles are launched into the between. "*All understanding is dialogical*," Voloshinov argues. "Understanding seeks a *counter-word* to the speaker's word" (*Marksizm* 104). It is important to note that the counterword comes not only from the other pole but from the between; it is a response not only to an interlocutor but to the word itself. When Bakhtin says that the word is shaped not only by what is said but by what is needed (*Dialogic* 280), he has in mind the counterword that is always yet to come, always a second coming. In the act of speaking and hearing, I am displaced, hurled into the between, into the word, where I encounter the silence of the yet-to-be and there move into the realm of the counterword.

Here it should be emphasized that in dialogue the listener and the speaker simultaneously seek a counterword or a response to the word. As Bakhtin expresses it in "The Problem of Verbal Genres," "the speaker himself is situated in precisely such an actively responsive understanding; he awaits not a passive understanding . . . but a response" (*Estetika* 247). We hear ourselves speak and respond to what we hear, so that the response is sought not only from the other but from the self as other. It is the word's bond to the between that makes it possible for a person to become other to himself. Every word calls for a reply, calls for a self, and the call of a given word issues from the between, from the atmosphere of discourse, standing and outstanding, out of which both speaker and listener, I and other, draw their breath, their presence, and their consciousness. Living consciousness is responsive consciousness, and human presence is presence in the dialogical word, where the human being is always beside himself. Consciousness is a coming before the countenance, before the face that speaks. Remember Levinas's declaration that "face and discourse are tied. The face speaks. It speaks, it is in this that it renders possible and begins all discourse. I have just refused the notion of vision to describe the authentic relationship with the other; it is discourse and, more exactly, response or responsibility which is this authentic relationship" (*Ethics* 87-88). Face and the between are tied. Both take the man who has a face outside of himself and turn him over to the word that transforms difference into nonindifference.

"A man never coincides with himself," Bakhtin writes in *Problems of Dostoevsky's Poetics*. "The genuine life of the personality takes place at the point of non-coincidence between a man and himself. . . . The genuine life of the personality is made available only through a *dialogic* penetration of that personality" (59). In these words we have still another expression of the between: it is the point where lip touches lip, pen touches paper, word touches word—the point of noncoincidence, which is always a point *between*. The genuine life of the personality is lived in the rite of passage through the between; dialogical penetration takes place in the between, where the man passes through himself in the return to himself from the other. In the genuine life of the personality *within* and *between* are synonyms. As Levinas puts it, "The privilege of the other in relation to the I—or the moral consciousness—is the very opening to exteriority, which is also an opening to highness" ("Signature" 185). The human being lives *within* the relation *between* I and the other; the human being lives in the word, in the house of being. Seeking a response, listener and speaker seek themselves as one who is in situation, engaged in dialogical interaction and self-penetration. Inasmuch as their interaction is indeed dialogical, each seeks the one thing needful, the needful word, which must come from the between of the relation and for which I am responsible. In this seeking, the I and the other struggle to answer the summons that comes from the between and that puts to each of them the question put to the first man: Where are you? And the needful response is a "here" that launches me into the between.

Where I am is what I mean. My ability to respond to the question is my ability to offer meaning and therefore to have meaning. The between is a question mark, not an exclamation point. In his "Notes from 1970-1971," Bakhtin observes that meaning is a response to a question (*Estetika* 350). Meaning, in other words, is dialogical; dialogue is animated by the questions that fuel it, not by the answers that bring it to a halt. Meaninglessness comes with the loss of questions, not the loss of answers. What launches us into the between is the quest; what we encounter in the between is the question. The word thus makes itself heard as a question; if every word seeks a reply, it is because every word harbors a question, and this is what gives discourse meaning. Hence it is possible to organize a game show in which the respondents must provide the question that goes with a given assertion and bestows meaning upon it. What we say and hear, then, is sense, not sound. "In fact," Voloshinov declares, "we never pronounce or hear the word; rather, we hear truth or lie, good or evil, important or unimportant, pleasant or unpleasant, and so on" (*Marksizm* 71). This invisibility of the word constitutes the visibility of the between, which is "seen" in an act of responsive understanding, where "I see" becomes "I understand." Foucault expresses this idea by saying, "The sign does not wait in silence for the coming of a man capable of recognizing it: it can be constituted only by an act of knowing" (*Order* 59); and later he adds, "It is in one and the same movement that the mind speaks and knows" (86). A word or sign is not an object, not a thing, but an event. Like a song, it becomes what it is in the singing of it.

In this regard, however, we must bear in mind one other statement from *Marxism and the Philosophy of Language:* "Meaning is not in the word or in the soul of the speaker or in the soul of the listener. Meaning is the *effect of the interaction between speaker and listener within the material of a given sound complex*" (Voloshinov, *Marksizm* 104). It would be more accurate to say that meaning is the *process* rather than the *effect*, of interaction; meaning is not simply the goal but is the way as well. The term *material*, too, may be misleading. "For the word is not a material thing," Bakhtin insists in *Problems of Dos-*

toevsky's Poetics, "but rather the eternally mobile, eternally fickle medium of dialogic interaction. It never gravitates towards a single consciousness or a single voice. The life of the word is contained in its transfer from one mouth to another, from one context to another context" (202). The life of the word unfolds in the between of the passage from context to context; the rite of passage is a passage through the between. The life of the word, further, is the life of meaning, and meaning is the life of life, the being and reality of life's attachment to life. Where does that reality, that being, reside? Heidegger offers a suggestion: "Being, as itself, spans its own province, which is marked off (*temnein,* *tempus*) by Being's being present in the word. Language is the precinct (*templum*), that is, the house of Being" (*Poetry* 132). Note the phrase "Being spans." Being, like the word, is *between*; present in the word, being is present in the between.

BEING AND THE BETWEEN

In *Marxism and the Philosophy of Language,* Voloshinov argues that the reality of the word resides between individuals (*Marksizm* 19), and reality is precisely the reality of the word. Or better: the reality that is, is born of the word. Clark and Holquist explain Bakhtin's view of this interrelation by saying, "The systematic aspects of language are to speech as the material world is to mind. Thus they differ from each other but always operate together. The two sets of features interact in a dynamic unity and cannot without conceptual violence be separated from each other. The arena where they intermingle and the force that binds them are both what Bakhtin understands by 'utterance' " (222). As Heidegger expresses it, "where the word fails, there is no thing" (*Unterwegs* 163). In the beginning is the word: first we have the world of words, and then the world of things falls into place. The word is not in space and time, but rather space and time are in the word, or between word and word. The world of things arises in the transfer of the word from mouth to mouth, never seen but always voiced. In the beginning, therefore, is the between, for the world of words and its concurrent reality are, again, between speaker and listener. Each time we are summoned to respond to the word, we are called into being, into the between, into the beginning. And as we respond, we call forth a world. In the life of one who lives in the word, everything, all of being, forever begins and never ends. For one who lives in the word is forever on the threshold, in a process of passage; reality is just such a passage from summons to response, from here to there. As Levinas has pointed out, "Here I am" means "Send me" (*Otherwise* 199). Send me over the threshold and into the between; launch me into being, where my testimony will instill me with reality. The word is both the vessel and carrier of being, and between the two lies the reality, the personality, of the self. The penetration of personality, then, is not only dialogical but is ontological as well: it is a bonding of word and being, and the bond is the between.

We should recall at this point a statement that Bakhtin makes in his book on Dostoevsky. Quoting Dostoevsky, he writes, " 'Reality in its entirety is not to be exhausted by what is immediately at hand, for an overwhelming part of this reality is contained in the form of a still *latent, unuttered future Word* " (90). To say that the future is *not yet* is to declare that it is forever beginning; it is the silence that answers before it is called and that calls as it answers. Such is the "latent, unuttered future Word." And the realm of the future word is the silent but eloquent between. If every word calls for a reply, it also calls forth a reality that emerges from the silence of the between. And because every word calls for a reply, reality is forever unfinished; it lies not only in what is uttered but in what is forever on the threshold of utterance. On the threshold, in the between, the soul of the word abides as the carrier of meaning and the vessel of memory that rushes ahead of itself, silently, to raise up the reality of a world. "Dasein's past," Heidegger writes, "does not *follow* it but rather goes ahead of it" (*Sein* 20). Why? Because the reality of its past is called forth by the *latent* word, already there but *not yet* uttered. Reality is not to be exhausted by what is immediately at hand, because it is constantly, silently thrown into the between, which is not yet determined.

If silence speaks, it bespeaks a reality. Or, in the words of Heidegger, "the call speaks in the uncanny mode of silence" (*Sein* 277), arising from within the word and from beyond it. Silence is the sound of possibility; for silence, everything, all being, is possible. If the word frames a reality, silence opens up an unbounded reality. A distinction is called for here: reality framed is the world, while open and unbounded reality is being. In the proposition that being is made of possibility lies an important aspect of its linkage with the between. For the between is constituted both by the framework of encounter and by the open-endedness of possibility. In this sense, being and the between form what Heidegger refers to as the Open. We have already used the language of "calling forth" or "bringing forth" with respect to the relation between being and the word. Here we may call to mind Heidegger's assertion that "the bringing forth places this being in the Open in such a way that what is to be brought forth clears the openness of the Open into which it comes forth" (*Poetry* 62). Reality clears the way for being, not the other way around; the formed posits the unbounded. But if, as Heidegger asserts, "language alone brings what is, as something that is, into the Open" (*Poetry* 73), so too does silence as unuttered discourse; silence becomes a mode of speaking, a clearing opened up by the framing of the word. "Only in genuine speaking is real silence possible," Heidegger declares. "In order to be able to be silent, Dasein must have something to say" (*Sein* 165). Reality is the reality of the silence that inhabits the word. Think of the silence of Abraham on the way to Moriah or the silence of Jesus before Pilate. The reality and truth of both lie in the resolve of their silence. It happens that the more I speak, the more I drain myself of truth; it happens that the one who truly shouts is the one who is about to explode with the word and yet remains silent.

It must also be noted that, contrary to what may seem to be the case at first glance, the Open—infinite and unbounded—is the between; what is limited lies in the speaker and in the listener. If "the infinity of the infinite lives in going backwards," as Levinas says (*Otherwise* 12), the place to which it returns is the between. The infinity of being, of unuttered and yet-to-be-uttered reality, teems in the between, where it finds its way into the finite, into the human realm. Bakhtin draws an important distinction: "In stillness there is no sound (or nothing makes a sound); in silence no one says anything (or no one speaks). Silence is possible only in the human realm (only for human being)" (*Estetika* 338). And because silence is possible only in the human realm, being is possible only in the human realm, which is the place of the world. What Heidegger says in his book on Hölderlin is true: "Only where language is, is there world" (35), because only where language is, is there silence between two, an unbounded space where the world of reality and the reality of the world jut up. This action of jutting up is what Heidegger means when he says, "The world never 'is'; it 'worlds' " (*Essense* 103). As the site of encounter, the path that leads into the world is itself the world; the world happens in the passage that posits it. The word "there" constitutes the road; and the chronotope of the road, which, Bakhtin points out, is a constitutive feature of literature's dialogical dimensions (*Dialogic* 98), is the chronotope of the between.

Only where there is Dasein or "being there" is there world. Being there, moreover, entails relationship within a structure, so that being there means being with. Dasein ex-sists ex-statically; it is where it is not, present by its absence. Recall Lacan's observation that "through the word—already a presence made of absence—absence itself comes to giving itself a name" (*Language* 39). And its name is Dasein. Two points should be noted in this connection: first, Dasein, or the living individual, encounters the reality of himself by way of relation to something other than himself; second, his relation to what is other turns on the word, on a process of speaking and hearing. Existence occurs, therefore, both within and outside the existing individual because the existing individual is a speaking individual. The structure within which encounter takes place is the dialogical structure of language; the setting is always language, from which the coordinates of space and time are derived. Thus we hear Heidegger saying, "Speech is a constitutive feature of Dasein's existence as an existential condition for the disclosure of Dasein" (*Sein* 161). Disclosure is the opening up, the clearing, of the between through the word; where being takes the form of existence, it takes the form of word. For the living individual, then, being there means having a voice; his existence is the existence of his voice as a response to another voice. The thing he is with is another voice. And so, Bakhtin declares, "two voices is the minimum for life, the minimum for existence" (*Problems* 252). Where there is being, there are two voices; again, one does not imply two, but rather two are required to make one. The existence of one voice rests on a relation to the other, which is to say, it rests on the between. Where there is being, there is the between.

Because being is rooted in relation, it is not something given but something generated, not something we have but something we achieve. Where the between is lost, relation fails, and instead of being we have the nothingness of isolation. This miscarriage occurs wherever the Thou who is the other voice is reduced to an It through what Heidegger terms "the saying work of the still covetous vision of things" (*Poetry* 128). If the silence of the between, of the I toward the Thou, is the house of being, then the muteness of the It, as still as a stone, is the place of nothingness. What Heidegger calls "the saying work of the still covetous vision of things" is precisely the unsaying stillness of the It. "The hard thing," he goes on to state, "is to accomplish existence. The hard thing consists not only in the difficulty of forming the work of language, but in the difficulty of going over from the saying work of the still covetous vision of things, from the work of the eyes, to the 'work of the heart' " (*Poetry* 128).

The work of the heart is the work of the between, where the word goes about the work of calling forth. To say that the hard thing to accomplish is existence is to express the difficulty of making silence speak from the heart. The needful thing to accomplish is existence in a movement inward, toward the "man within the man," where we encounter the love that constitutes relation. "The inner and invisible domain of the heart," Heidegger insists, "is not only more inward than the interior that belongs to calculating representation, and therefore more invisible; it also extends further than does the realm of merely producible objects. Only in the invisible innermost of the heart is man inclined toward what there is for him to love" (*Poetry* 127-28). What is there for man to love? The other with whom he is joined in the creation of the between as the realm of being. In what may be regarded as a free translation of Heidegger's statement, Bakhtin writes, "Only in communion, in the interaction of one person with another, can the 'man in man' be revealed, for others as well as for oneself" (*Problems* 252). Again, between and within are synonyms; the between is the sameness of the other and the oneself, what Levinas calls "the other in the same" (*Otherwise* 25). To exist is to love. For love is the stuff of being. Void of love, we live in the void.

It is important here not to confuse love with feelings. Our feelings lurk within us, like ghosts in a machine, but we live in our love, just as we live in the air, by the breath we draw from the air; it is the thread upon which the pearls of our world are strung. What is the being that comes to life in the between? It is the love between I and Thou. Thus being arises more through passion than through thought, more in the flame of revelation than in the form of speculation. Speculation is the "calculating representation," the "work of the eyes," cited by Heidegger above; revelation is the "work of the heart," inclined toward what there is to love. The thing revealed is the between, out of which comes the word with its summons and response that signify the presence of the two voices of relation. Hence we find Bakhtin saying, "The idea *lives* not in one person's *isolated* individual consciousness—if it remains there only, it degenerates and dies. The idea begins to live . . . only when it enters into genuine dialogic relationships with other ideas, with the ideas of *others*" (*Problems* 87-88). If love is not a feeling, however, neither is it an idea. Rather, it is the life force, the soul, of the idea. There is no dialogical relation without love, just as there is no love in isolation. Love is dialogic.

Having said this much, we can see that love is the soul, the affirming flame, of the word when we hear Bakhtin add, "The idea is a *live event*, played out at the point of dialogic meeting between two or several consciousnesses. In this sense the idea is similar to the *word*, with which it is dialogically united. Like the word, the idea wants to be heard, understood, and 'answered' by other voices from other positions. Like the word, the idea is by nature dialogic" (88). This is why Bakhtin asserts, "Only the unfinalized and inexhaustible 'man in man' can become a man of the idea" (*Problems* 86). For the "man in man" is the love within the man, inexhaustible because it is unfinalized, unfinalized because it is dialogical, forever in a process of hearing and response. The idea is a live event whenever it is the issue not of rumination but of passion; it is love that dialogically weds word and idea. Love is a question mark, not an exclamation point. It wants to be heard and understood because such is the way in which what is offered is received and thus revealed. It is the hunger Levinas speaks of when he says, "The emptiness of hunger is emptier than all curiosity, cannot be compensated for with the mere hearing of what it demands" (*Otherwise* 72). The living idea of dialogical relation, then, is not speculative but revelatory; being is not thought—it is revealed between two. Like the living idea, being is dialogical; being is love.

The thing that obscures the between and thus threatens being is isolated speculation, what Heidegger describes as "the evil and keenest danger" when he says, "The evil and thus keenest danger is thinking itself. It must think against itself, which it can only seldom do" (*Poetry* 8). Yet, Heidegger points out, "it may be that any other salvation than that which comes from *where the* danger is, is still within the unholy" (*Poetry* 118). What, then, is required for thinking to think against itself, against the threat of nothingness? Passionate resolve. The thinker must think with and through his wounds: the between is a wound, and being is born from that wound, which opens up in resolve. "*Esse* is *interesse;* essence is interest," as Levinas has argued (*Otherwise* 4), and resolve is born of interest, of inter-essence. This resolve is thus the substance of being and the support of the between. It is what Heidegger calls *will* when he says, "The Being of beings is the will. The will is the self-concentrating gathering of every *ens* unto itself. Every being, as a being, is in the will. It *is* as something willed. This should be taken as saying: that which is, is not first and only as something willed; rather, insofar as it is, it is itself in the mode of will. Only by virtue of being willed is each being that which, in its own way, does the willing in the will" (*Poetry* 100-101). Just as there is no separating the dancer from the dance, so is the human being of a piece with the will to be. It is the will that launches the individual into the between—between himself and the other, between his *is* and his *yet-to-be.* The categories of meaning and purpose that Bakhtin associates with the *not yet* (*Estetika* 109) exist by virtue of the will. The will pits me against myself and produces the wounds by which I am recognized and through which I enter the wound of the between. It is at once a rending and a healing, refusal and affirmation, the fuel that propels the individual in a process of action and reaction through the rite of passage.

The movement of gathering myself into myself, through the will that is my being, is a movement toward the between, where I hammer out my being through my power of relation. Joining my *is* with my *not yet,* I am what I will to become, and the process of becoming that characterizes being occurs in the between. Conceived of as will or resolve, then, I am *not yet* what I am; the project of forging myself is forever incomplete, forever in question. If my thought is to think against itself, I must refuse the temptation to what Heidegger calls tranquilization (*Sein* 347), or coming to a stop. When thought fails to think against itself, the deadly result is a curling up in the cave of sleep. To think against oneself is to maintain the conflicts of consciousness, conflicts that are the issue of resolve or will. Further, because I am one whose being is grounded in resolve, I am responsible for what I become or fail to become. An essential feature of my being, therefore, is the ability to be guilty. Indeed, this is why Heidegger defines guilt in terms of resolve by saying, "This distinctive and authentic disclosedness to which Dasein bears witness through its conscience—*the casting of itself into its ownmost being-guilty, silently and in anguish*—is what we call resolve" (*Sein* 296-97). I am guilty to the extent that I fail to achieve a dialogical presence in the between through lack of resolve. And there is no getting it over with. I leap into the abyss only to land again on its edge and find myself lacking. Where resolve is absent, so is the word, so is the between, so is being. This lack, in short, is nothingness, and the thing that announces it is dread.

Thus we hear Heidegger saying, "Dread opens up nothingness" and "steals the word away from us" (*Wegmarken* 9). When dread eclipses resolve, the idle talk of *das man*, or the They, takes over the word of the individual, so that he is no longer dwelling in the between of being but is languishing in the void of nothingness, no longer speaking but spoken. Here we may recall Bakhtin's remark in *The Dialogic Imagination*, where he says, "The word in language is half someone else's. It becomes 'one's own' only when the speaker populates it with his own intention" (293). Where Bakhtin writes *intention* we may read *resolve*; it is the tensing in, the gathering of oneself unto oneself through the will. When the word becomes one's own, one establishes a presence through the word. In resolve, then, the individual becomes the place of the word, and the between becomes the place of the individual: being is achieved when the word is spoken with one's whole being. The human being offers himself in the word he offers to another human being and thus becomes who he is. Perhaps the highest example of the word spoken with one's whole being is the example invoked earlier:

prayer. In prayer we gauge the between as *between God and man,* and "only in this Between," Heidegger writes, "is it decided as to who man is and where his existence lies" (*Erläuterungen* 43). And this between is there, whenever the between is there; when word and being are joined, the word is prayer, and being is the between. Hence the relation between human beings—the relation that constitutes being—entails a relation to a third, through whom the measure of the between is taken.

THE THIRD

In *Aesthetics of Verbal Art* Bakhtin writes, "Every dialogue proceeds as though against the background of a responsive understanding of a Third who is invisibly present, standing above all the participants in the dialogue. . . . The Third referred to here has nothing to do with mysticism or metaphysics. . . . It is a constitutive feature of the whole expression" (*Estetika* 306). There is no "whole expression," no joining of word and being into a whole, without the Third; the Third is the wholeness of the horizon that encompasses all horizons, otherwise than being and beyond essence. Herein lies its invisibility. It is the invisibility Levinas describes when he says, "When in the presence of the other I say 'Here I am!', this 'Here I am!' is the place through which the Infinite enters into language, but without giving itself to be seen. Since it is not thematized, in any case originally, it does not appear. The 'invisible God' is not to be understood as God invisible to the senses, but as God non-thematizable in thought, and nonetheless as non-indifferent to the thought which is not thematization" (*Ethics* 106).

Beyond all themes, all limitations, the Third is the one for whom all things are possible, the infinite expanse of possibility for summons and response. As such, it is the unfinalized truth, which sustains the way of the dialogue and the movement in the between. One will recall once again Lacan's invocation of the Other, a concept that resembles this notion of the Third, when he says, "Who, then, is this other to whom I am more attached than to myself, since, at the heart of my assent to my own identity it is still he who agitates me? . . . This other is the Other that even my lie invokes as a guarantor of the truth in which it subsists. By which we can also see that it is with the appearance of language that the dimension of truth emerges" (*Écrits* 172). Conceived in terms of the relation to the Third, the truth is not so much what we know but what we are and where we are moving. The Third is the presence that abounds in the open-ended between, what Heidegger refers to as "the gods" when he asserts that "the word takes on its naming power only when the gods bring us to language" (*Erläuterungen* 42). Here we may recall Kenneth Burke's remark that "statements that great theologians have made about the nature of 'God' might be adapted *mutatis mutandis* for use as purely secular observations on the nature of *words*" (1-2). In his capacity for naming—for linking word and thing—man is a creature created in the image of God. If language is the house of being, the Third is the builder of the house.

The house is the place of dwelling, and dwelling is a matter that entails two, an I and a Thou, whose presence before each other is a presence before a Third. The Third is the definitive feature of the dialogical relation generated by the word. It has been noted that two are required to form one; here let it be said that three are needed to constitute two. The word, therefore, is transindividual, to use Bakhtin's term, and it consists of three elements: "The word (any sign in general) is transindividual. Everything said or expressed lies outside the 'soul' of the speaker and does not belong to him. . . . The author (speaker) has his inalienable rights to the word, but his rights are also the listener's rights; his rights are the rights of those whose voices resound in the word offered by the author. . . . The word is a drama in which three characters participate (not a duet but a trio)" *(Estetika* 300-301). It will be recalled that Clark and Holquist identify the three characters in the dialogical interaction as the speaker, the listener, and the topic (205). But "topic" is too weak, even misleadingly so. In place of "topic" we should say *truth*. For the relation between two is dialogical only insofar as it is characterized by an interest and a stake in truth. In truth lies the life of I and Thou, the substance of the word, and the essence of being. Truth is the *living* presence that makes the idea a *live event*, as Bakhtin describes it (*Problems* 88). It is the one to whom we answer in the light of the "higher responsibility" of which we have heard Bakhtin speak (*Estetika* 179).

Indeed, the Third is the definitive element of responsibility; responsibility is accountability to the Third.

The speaker, again, is not Adam, not the first to disturb the silence of the universe. His every utterance is replete with a host of words within the word, with the presence of the Other who listens and summons from within and from beyond, from the between. The Other, the Third, is what Bakhtin deems the "over-I" when in his "Notes from 1970-1971" he writes, "The overman, the over-*I*— that is, the witness and judge of every man (of every *I*)—is therefore not a human being but the *Other*" (*Estetika* 342). When word and being are joined in their wholeness, they form the Other, who is also the process of the joining and is the one from whom the call to accountability issues. It is because the Third calls that we have dialogue. In *Being and Time* Heidegger alludes to the call of the Other when he states that "the call comes *from* me and from *beyond* me" (275), and that "the call is . . . something like an *alien* voice" (277); alien because it interferes with my voice and with the voice of the other. The alien voice is what continually takes the word elsewhere, turning it inside out and opening up the path of dialogue. The voice speaks not so much from the word but from between word and word; it speaks not so much in the mouth of the one or the other but in the transfer from mouth to mouth.

It was suggested above that *between* and *within* are synonyms; now we may go a step further—or a step back—and say that *within* and *beyond* are synonyms, calling to mind Heidegger's statement that "the midst of two is inwardness" (*Unterwegs* 24). Inwardness here is best understood as the inwardness Levinas speaks of when he says, "The exteriority of the Infinite becomes somehow an inwardness in the sincerity of a witness borne. . . . Inwardness is not a secret place somewhere in me; it is that reverting in which the eminently exterior, precisely in virtue of this eminent exteriority, this impossibility of being contained and consequently entering into a theme, forms, as infinity, an exception to essence, concerns me and circumscribes me and orders me by my own voice. The command is stated by the mouth of him it commands" (*Otherwise* 147). The midst is the beyond, and the beyond is the Third or the Other, who is closer to us than our innermost selves, within and beyond.

The call to being thus comes from the Third; the Third is the origin of being and of the word. As Heidegger has said, it beckons in the uncanny mode of silence (*Sein* 277), in what Levinas calls "preoriginary saying" when he says, "In proximity, in signification, in my giving of signs, already the infinite speaks through the witness I bear of it, in my sincerity, in my saying without said, preoriginary saying which is said in the mouth of the very one that receives the witness" (*Otherwise* 151). The Third summons us to the presence generated by the word, and it is an alien voice because our presence is always in question, always lacking, always—like truth—somewhere else. This is why the Third is the judge, as well as the witness, of every being who says "I" only to lose to language the very thing he voices. This is why every I stands in a relation not only to a Thou but to a Third, an eternal Thou, who dwells between I and Thou. There is no relation of an I to a Thou without the relation of the I to the Third, who addresses the I through the Thou and to whom the I responds by answering the Thou. Whatever we do to the least of our brothers, we do to the Third. When the relation to the Third fails, we fail to attain being and are turned over to nothingness; when that relation fails, we lose the light of the between and dangle in the darkness of the abyss. And when does that relation fail? It fails when I "simply accept the values of my particular time and place, which is an avoidance of activity that has the effect of making my life a subfunction of a self-imposed 'axiological reflex' (*cennostnyj refleks,* similar to Heidegger's *das Man*)" (Clark and Holquist 76). It fails when I fail to speak the word with my whole being; when I fall from dialogical relation to monological recitation, calculation, and negotiation; when I have lost the question and strayed from the quest that moves me toward the truth; when I am lured into the sediment of the fixed phrases and ready answers that become my tomb.

The relation to the Third constitutes the precarious presence— the word and being—of the I by bringing the I to the threshold, to the site of the between. If language speaks, as Heidegger has said, "by calling the one summoned into the dif-ference of the between" (*Unterwegs* 28), the Third is the one who announces in language the absolute difference—and absolute nonindifference. It is the relation to the Third, in other words, that makes the threshold of the between the place of crisis. This relation is an important part of

Bakhtin's concern with Dostoevsky, for example, and it leads him to see in Dostoevsky what Heidegger never fully brings out in the German poets. Says Bakhtin, "Dostoevsky always represents a person *on the threshold* of a final decision, at a moment of *crisis*, at an unfinalizable—and *unpredeterminable*—turning point for his soul" (*Problems* 61). In *The Dialogic Imagination* we read, "Discourse lives, as it were, on the boundary" (284), and the boundary is made of decision. The threshold of decision is the threshold of relation; to live dialogically is to live decisively, where decisiveness is gauged by the Third and is the measure of the substance and resolve of the soul.

What, then, is the soul? Bakhtin offers a cryptic definition in "Author and Hero": "The soul is spirit unrealized for itself, reflected in the loving consciousness of another (person, God)" (*Estetika* 98). Where Bakhtin writes "person, God" we may read "Thou, Third." In the first section of this chapter we invoked the image of polarity as a metaphor for the presence that pulsates in the between. With Bakhtin's concept of the soul and his notion of the Third, we may identify that polarity as spirit. The task of becoming present before another—Thou, Third—is the task of transforming matter into spirit, of generating a presence that is never finished but forever fulfilled. If, as Heidegger claims, the between is the measure gauged between God and man (*Erläuterungen* 43), the thing that gauges the measure is the spirit or the love of the loving consciousness, the love that must love all the more. Such a responsive consciousness toward the Thou arises only when it is also a consciousness of the Third.

In "Author and Hero" Bakhtin goes on to say that "the soul is the gift of my spirit to the *Other*" (*Estetika* 116). Again, we may understand the Other to be the Third and spirit, moreover, to be love. Like love, the soul is mine only to the extent that I am able to give it to another (person, God), and I offer my soul to the Third by offering it to a Thou, to the human being before me, with whom I am gathered in the name of the Third. To be gathered with another in the name of the Third is to offer and receive the word uttered in love and in gratitude. If we remember Heidegger's assertion that the word arises in gratitude, as the echo of the kindness or favor of being (*Wegmarken* 105), we see more clearly that here, in gratitude, lies the word's connection with being. Freely translated, every word uttered dialogically, in affirmation and response, means "thank you." And the "you" of this "thank you" is both the Thou and the Third. The word is not the vessel of being; rather, being rises up in the offering and receiving of the word between I and Thou, between I and the nameless Third. The *event* of giving and receiving, of responding and hearing, is spirit; it is the movement of a constant return to myself by way of the Third. In short, it is the movement of becoming that distinguishes spiritual life. Since my spiritual life is characterized by this movement, I am never coincident with myself. As Bakhtin expresses it in *Problems of Dostoevsky's Poetics*, "a man never coincides with himself. One cannot apply to him the formula A = A" (59). Why? Because to be a human being is to be a dialogical being, forever called into being through responsive interaction. To be a human being is to be a spiritual being.

In order for a man to penetrate himself, he must go through the Third or "the witness and judge of every man" (*Estetika* 342). In the light of what has been said about the relation to the Third, we can see that the mediating role of the Third creates a tension between the soul and spirit. Bakhtin brings out this tension when he says, "The soul is an image of the totality of all that is truly experienced, of all that is at hand, in the soul in time; the spirit, however, is the totality of all meaningful significance and direction in life, of all acts issuing from itself" (*Estetika* 97-98). One way to describe the tension between soul and spirit, then, is to say it is the tension between time and eternity. The moment of crisis Bakhtin refers to above in his remark about Dostoevsky's characters is a point of contact between time and eternity, between what is lived and what is meaningful, between soul and spirit. The I-to-Thou relation is a soul-to-soul relation, one that takes on meaning in the light of the soul-to-spirit relation. "Wherever there are two of us," Bakhtin notes, "the important thing . . . is not that without me there is *still one such* human being . . . but that, for me, he is *another*" (*Estetika* 78). Here, again, *another* includes the Thou and the Third. It is not that there are two betweens but that the two relationships constitute the single between where word and being take place.

As the witness and judge of every man, the Third both weighs and reveals the constant disparity between the totality of all that is at hand and the totality of all that is meaningful. The weighing is itself the revealing; the totality of the all is nestled in the particular: this is the meaning of the Third. Because the Third is there, the disparity is there; which is to say, because the Third is there, the difference of nonindifference is there. And because the disparity is there, "the definition given to me lies not in the categories of temporal being," Bakhtin asserts, "but in the categories of the *not-yet-existing*, in the categories of purpose and meaning, in the meaningful future, which is at odds with anything I have in the past or present. To be myself for myself means yet becoming myself (*to cease becoming myself . . . means spiritual death*)" (*Estetika* 109). Stated differently, I am defined in terms of possibility. The Third does not represent the paralysis of predetermination but the open-endedness of possibility: I am defined in terms of the Third. The ultimate word between I and Thou is thus forever yet to be uttered, and the relation between I and the Third is forever unsettled. The Third is the elsewhere of word and being that transforms my proximity to the Thou into a distance or an absolute difference, a rift that I have yet to bridge. As in physics, time here is a dimension of space: the categories of the not-yet-existing constitute the spatiality of relation. *Not yet*—more, always more—is the watchword of the Eternal as well as the Infinite.

Looking to Heidegger's remarks about the *not yet* of Dasein, we may now view the Third not only in terms of possibility but of potentiality. Says Heidegger, "If the existence of the being of Dasein is determined and its essence partly constituted by its potentiality for being, then as long as it exists as such a potentiality Dasein must *not yet be* something" (*Sein* 233). Heidegger's "potentiality for being" may be understood as Bakhtin's "all meaningful significance and direction," that is, may be understood from the position of the Third. The Third holds sway over the something that I am not yet. As long as I exist, the meaning *of* my life is in question, and the meaning *in* my life rests on the movement I make toward what I am not yet; that is to say, the meaning in my life is grounded in my relation to the Third, which is the realm of spirit and of my spiritual life, the realm of the between. In this relation I find my depth; living in the spirit, to use Bakhtin's words, "I live in the depth of myself through faith and hope in the ongoing possibil-

ity of the inner miracle of a new birth" (*Estetika* 112). For the
potentiality of what I am not yet is the potentiality of a new birth.
And the seed of that new birth lies in faith. Here we see the eternal
face and facet of the Third: inasmuch as my being is grounded in a
dialogical relation to the Third via the Thou, I may say, "I am that
I am not yet." Levinas makes this point by saying, "The return is
sketched out in the going, the appeal is understood in the response,
the 'provocation' coming from God is in my invocation, gratitude
is already gratitude for this state of gratitude" (*Otherwise* 149). He
who says "I" with all his being—meaning I who am for Thou, who
am for the Third—becomes the link between word and being. He
becomes, in short, the between, the place of the new birth.

Who or what is the new being I am born into? It is the Third,
Spirit or God, if you will. Or better: it is God as absolute love.
Better still: it is the absolute expression of God's love in the God-
man or the Christ. "For," Lacan points out, "I can only just prove
to the Other that he exists, not, of course, with the proofs for the
existence of God, with which over the centuries he has been killed
off, but by loving him, a solution introduced by the Christian
kerygma" (*Écrits* 317). In the appeal to the Christ, of course, we have
perhaps the most radical point of difference between Bakhtin and
Heidegger. In the Christ, Bakhtin writes, "for the first time appears an infinitely profound *I-for-myself*, . . . immeasurably good to
the other, rendering the whole truth to the other, revealing and
confirming in all its fullness the precious originality of the other"
(*Estetika* 51). In this way the Christ brings us the revelation of God
and of man. For Bakhtin, Clark and Holquist explain, "Christ is
important for revealing for the first time the basis of all human
consciousness and thus for supplying the key to understanding all
things human" (86). Later on they note, "This conviction that the
sign has a body corresponds to Bakhtin's ontotheological view that
the spirit has a Christ. The kenotic event that is reenacted in
language is the mode of God's presence to human beings" (225).
The Christ reveals the I-for-myself that constitutes my highest
potentiality for being. He is the one who summons me from his
third position to a new birth through a relation to the other, to the
Thou. Hence Bakhtin realizes that "that which I must be for the
other is what God is for me" (*Estetika* 52). But I am never yet what I

must be for the other. The truth and the word I offer are never quite whole, and I am constantly between myself and the other, myself and the Third. Once again it is from the depths of this between that being must be continually reaffirmed and resurrected through the relation of the I to the Thou, of the I to the Third, a relation that inheres in the word.

Bakhtin and Heidegger help us to see that the between is the seat of word and being; it is the realm of spirit, where word and being are one. The task that faces human being is to move into that realm, to respond to the summons that comes from the Third, who is both within and beyond, both now and yet to be. The task that faces human being is to become whole in the relation to another (person, God) that opens the way to the between. The task is to become present in an apotheosis of presence, so that when we are called we may answer, as Abraham answered, "Here I am," where *here* is *between.* And it is a matter of spiritual life or spiritual death.

How can we make sense of this? Where can we point and say, "There is the between"? Nowhere. And everywhere. Or the inner somewhere, which, the intellect wants to declare, is nowhere. We cannot say that the between is in this place or that place but only that it is near, closer to us than we are to ourselves, and that in the saying itself the nearness of the between—of the spirit—is given. "The witness," as Levinas states it, "testifies to what was said by himself. For he has said 'Here I am!' before the Other; and from the fact that before the Other he recognizes the responsibility which is incumbent on himself, he has manifested what the face of the Other signified for him. The glory of the Infinite reveals itself through what it is capable of doing in the witness" (*Ethics* 109). In order to reach "the glory of the Infinite," we must set out, again, like Abraham, without knowing where we go, leaving behind all the calculation and fabrication we engage in whenever we attempt to create the illusion of a guarantee. In short, the movement into the between is a movement of faith. Thus we hear Bakhtin saying, "We can live and realize ourselves neither *with a guarantee* nor *in a void* but only *in faith.* Life (and consciousness) from within itself is nothing other than the realization of faith; the pure self-consciousness of life is the realization of faith" (*Estetika* 126-27). In a leap, suddenly, faith takes us into the between, where life finds its attachment to life in the wholeness of the I's relation to the Thou. For an instant eternity shows its face. Word and being announce themselves in a single voice, in the utterance of word and being: I Am That I Am.

SIX

Conclusion

At the outset of this volume it was stated that the essays it contains are as much an effort to understand as an attempt to explain. It is time to ask what we have understood. In our process of passage we have gone from one threshold to another. And so it is now: as we near the conclusion of the endeavor, we come not to an end but to a threshold. At the threshold, arriving at some kind of understanding is not a matter of settling on the right answer but of posing the right question. We must be careful not to make the end of the investigation the end of the dialogue, and dialogue lives by its questions, by its quest.

Beginning with the title—*Literature and Spirit*—this book has dealt with relationships, and its setting has been the *between* of those relationships. Both the method and the content have been dialogical, so that the linkage throughout has revolved around the word. We have seen how laughter, for example, is manifested in the word, how it questions the truth of discourse and affects the growth of literature. Madness has been described in terms of a "delirious discourse," the most alien form of the alien word, and Dostoevsky's dialogical novels have been found to be novels about the word. A poetics of the word, indeed, is a poetics of spirit, and the aesthetic endeavor is a spiritual endeavor. Thus, examining the author's creation of a hero through the word, we discovered that such a creative process is centered on the word as the language of the soul or self. It turned out, in fact, that the word involves the self in the deepest levels of signification through the self's response and responsibility to the other. In the relation to the other—a relation created and sustained by the word—the between is revealed; it is the place where being occurs as the offspring of relation. And the witness to the whole dialogical process, the one in whom the word finds its meaning, is spirit.

The questions we pose, the quest we undertake, and the connections we realize must be understood in the light of spirit. Literature carries on its dialogue with life in a struggle to give voice to truth inasmuch as literature is itself an expression of spirit. Responsibility to and for another human being frees the I for its offering to a Thou because this too is a manifestation of spirit that includes literary dimensions of signification and self-creation. That madness can both threaten and reveal, that one being can signify another, that dialogical relation can constitute a single presence, that silence itself can speak—all of this is a revelation of spirit. Indeed, all of this *is* spirit, the subjectivity of "the other in the same." Saint Augustine once declared that when we see God in the world, it is God who sees through our eyes. So it is with spirit. Only spirit can give voice to spirit; only spirit can inspirit or inspire, from within and from beyond. Spirit is always about itself, just as literature always has itself as its subject. In the language of spirit— which is a dialogical, that is to say, a literary language—I Am and Thou Art are synonymous. That the language of spirit thus turns back on itself points up the oneness of spirit and situates spirit in a third position between two. The spiritual word is a presence that decides the truth of the presence, of the interrelation, between I and Thou. In the parlance of the literary event, spirit makes every I, every Thou, into author, hero, and reader. It transforms every self into a literary text that comes to life in its utterance and is enriched as it is heard. In short, spirit turns life into literature and literature into life.

While language is the medium of literature, literature is the maker of language. As we have seen, literature is about itself, and its hero is the word. Just as the scene of the word is the between, so is the between the setting of literature. In literature, language speaks. What speaks has meaning to those who have ears that hear; and what speaks is literary. Where there is meaning, there is literature; for where there is literature, life is in dialogue with itself. Literature is the bond in life's attachment to life; it couples life with life to bring forth life in truth and in spirit. The dialogical word that has commanded our attention from the start is the literary word, the living word, the spiritual word. If the between is the setting for literature, it is because the between is the realm of life. If two voices are the minimum for life, so are they the minimum for literature. Literature is a unity comprising two, made of interrelation, constituted by the word offered and received by I and Thou. Or better: conceived as spirit, literature is the triangular or triune presence formed by I, Thou, and the Third. It is not situated at any single point but rather pulsates as the trinity itself, the one to which the three are equal. In literature, as in life, there is one who summons, one who responds, and one who bears witness. And the process is unending. The issue is always upon us, the question forever before us, the judgment eternally at hand.

The needful point must be made once more, making the end a repetition of the beginning, a new threshold: the task before us, in these pages and in leaving them behind, is to answer as we are called and declare, "Here I am!"

Works Cited

Bakhtin, Mikhail. *The Dialogic Imagination*. Trans. Caryl Emerson and Michael Holquist. Austin: Univ. of Texas Press, 1981.

———. *Estetika slovesnogo tvorchestva*. Moscow: Art, 1979.

———. *Esthétique et théorie du roman*. Trans. Daria Olivier. Paris: Gallimard, 1978.

———. *Problems of Dostoevsky's Poetics*. Trans. Caryl Emerson. Minneapolis: Univ. of Minnesota Press, 1984.

———. *Rabelais and His World*. Trans. Helene Isialsky. Cambridge, Mass.: MIT Press, 1968.

Berdyaev, Nicholas. *The Destiny of Man*. Trans. Natalie Duddington. New York: Harper and Row, 1960.

———. *Dostoevsky*. Trans. Donald Attwater. New York: New American Library, 1974.

Bernstein, Michael André. "When the Carnival Turns Bitter: Preliminary Reflections upon the Abject Hero." *Critical Inquiry* 10 (1983): 283-305.

Burke, Kenneth. *The Rhetoric of Religion: Studies in Logology*. Berkeley: University of California Press, 1970.

Clark, Katerina, and Michael Holquist. *Mikhail Bakhtin*. Cambridge, Mass.: Harvard Univ. Press, 1984.

Dostoevsky, F.M. *Besy*. Moscow: Government Publications in Art, 1957. Vol. 7 of *Sobranie sochinenii*. 10 vols. 1956-58.

———. *Brat'ya Karamazovy*. Petrozovodsk: Karelsky Book Publisher, 1970.

———. *Dvoinik*. Leningrad: Academy of Sciences, 1972. Vol. 1 of *Polnoe sobranie sochinenii*. 30 vols. 1972.

———. *Idiot*. Moscow: Government Publications in Art, 1958. Vol. 6 of *Sobranie sochinenii*. 10 vols. 1956-58.

———. *Neizdannyi Dostoevsky*. Moscow: "Science," 1971.

————. *Prestuplenie i nakazanie*. Moscow, 1982.

————. *Zapiski iz podpol'ya*. Leningrad: Academy of Sciences, 1973. Vol. 5 of *Polnoe sobranie sochinenii*. 30 vols. 1972–.

————. *Zapisnye tetradi F.M. Dostoevskogo*. Moscow: Academia, 1935.

Eliot, T.S. *The Waste Land and Other Poems*. New York: Harcourt Brace Jovanovich, 1962.

Emerson, Caryl. Preface. *Problems of Dostoevsky's Poetics*. By Mikhail Bakhtin. Trans. Emerson. Minneapolis: Univ. of Minnesota Press, 1984. xxiv-xliii.

————. "The Outer World and Inner Speech: Bakhtin, Vygotsky, and the Internalization of Language." *Critical Inquiry* 10 (1983): 245-64.

Felman, Shoshana. "Beyond Oedipus: The Specimen Story of Psychoanalysis." *MLN* 98 (1983): 1021-53.

————. "To Open the Question." *Yale French Studies* 55-56 (1977): 7.

Foucault, Michel. *The Archaeology of Knowledge and The Discourse on Language*. Trans. A.M. Sheridan Smith. New York: Pantheon Books, 1972.

————. *Madness and Civilization*. Trans. Richard Howard. New York: Pantheon Books, 1965.

————. *The Order of Things*. New York: Vintage Books, 1973.

Gide, André. *Dostoevsky*. Trans. Louise Varese. New York: New Directions, 1961.

Heidegger, Martin. *Erläuterungen zu Hölderlins Dichtung*. 2nd ed. Frankfurt am Main: Vittorio Klostermann, 1951.

————. *The Essence of Reasons*. Trans. Terrence Malick. Evanston, Ill.: Northwestern Univ. Press, 1969.

————. *Poetry, Language, Thought*. Trans. Albert Hofstadter. New York: Harper and Row, 1971.

————. *Sein und Zeit*. 2nd ed. Tübingen: Max Niemeyer, 1929.

————. *Unterwegs zur Sprache*. Tübingen: Neske, 1959.

————. *Wegmarken*. Frankfurt am Main: Vittorio Klostermann, 1967.

Lacan, Jacques. *Écrits*. Trans. Alan Sheridan. New York: Norton, 1977.

————. *The Language of the Self*. Trans. Anthony Wilden. Baltimore, Md.: The Johns Hopkins Univ. Press, 1968.

Levinas, Emmanuel. *Ethics and Infinity*. Trans. Richard A. Cohen. Pittsburgh: Duquesne Univ. Press, 1985.

———. *Otherwise than Being or Beyond Essence.* Trans. Alphonso Lingis. The Hague: Nijhoff, 1981.

———. "Signature." *Research in Phenomenology* 8 (1978): 175-89.

Nietzsche, Friedrich. *Also sprach Zarathustra* in *Werke*, Vol. 1. Munich: Carl Hanser Verlag, 1965-67.

Pascal, Blaise. *Pensées.* Trans. A.J. Krailsheimer. New York: Penguin, 1977.

Ragland-Sullivan, Ellie. "Lacan, Language, and Literary Criticism." *Literary Review* 24 (1981): 562-77.

Todorov, Tzvetan. *Mikhail Bakhtine: Le principe dialogique.* Paris: Éditions du Seuil, 1981.

Voloshinov, V.N. *Freudianism: A Marxist Critique.* Trans. I.R. Titunik. New York: Academic Press, 1976.

———. *Marksizm i filosofiya yazyka.* 2nd ed. Leningrad: Gosizdat, 1930.

Wilden, Anthony. "Lacan and the Discourse of the Other." *The Language of the Self.* By Jacques Lacan. Trans. Anthony Wilden. Baltimore, Md.: The Johns Hopkins Univ. Press, 1968. 197–311.

Index

monologism, 9, 21, 39-40, 52, 58, 127. *See also* reason
myth, 8

Nerval, Gérard de, 25
Nietzsche, Friedrich, 25, 28, 31
nonindifference, 47, 94-95, 129, 134, 135, 148, 151; and signification, 105, 108. *See also* resolve
nothingness, 24, 31, 100, 125, 141, 143, 148; and dread, 144
novel, the, 10, 14, 24-25, 35, 39, 40, 43, 50, 53, 69, 71, 73, 83, 86; and truth, 58, 60; and spirit, 90; and the Other, 92

open-endedness, 59, 77, 86, 132, 139, 151; and signification, 107
other, the, 17, 18, 19, 36, 37, 39, 51, 52, 54, 64, 99, 104, 107, 109, 111, 114, 118, 141, 145, 149; and freedom, 49-50; and truth, 56, 63; hero as, 80-89; and signification, 110; and subjectivity, 115; and the between, 129, 130, 152-53
Other, the, 70-72, 79, 88-95, 117, 122, 123, 124, 145-46, 147, 152. *See also* third position, truth

Pascal, Blaise, 22
personality, penetration of, 44-55, 109, 135, 138
Plato, 5, 17
polyglossia, 5
polyphony, 64; and form of the novel, 35-44
possibility, 7, 14, 59, 91, 124, 138-39, 145, 151
prayer, 79, 123, 132-33, 145
psyche, 104, 109, 111, 112, 121

Rabelais, François, 5, 6, 11, 128
reader, the, 29, 30, 96-97
reason, 8, 12, 14, 15, 35, 38. *See also* monologism
rebirth, 27, 28-29, 45, 64-65, 152, 153; and signification, 107
Renaissance, 10, 11, 13, 49
resolve, 73; and the between, 132; and being, 142-44
responsiblity, 28-31, 42, 44, 45, 47, 55-56, 57, 74, 75, 82, 85, 97, 98-99, 125, 129, 135, 144, 153; and freedom, 57-58, 122; and truth, 58; and vulnerability, 63, 120; and the Other, 93-94, 96, 118, 119; and meaning, 108; and dialogical relation, 109-19; and spirit, 123; and the between, 133-34; and the Third, 146-47
resurrection. *See* rebirth
return, movement of, 17, 26, 27, 132, 152
Rilke, Rainer Maria, 8, 128

Sade, Marquis de, 27, 28
self, 9, 42, 48, 65, 72, 90, 111, 138; and the other, 50, 52-54, 67, 69, 73, 74, 78, 79, 81-86, 112, 148; and the novel, 53; and discourse, 68-69, 82-83, 121; of the author, 72-80; and the Other, 92, 148; and signification, 102; and spirit, 119-23; and the between, 152. *See also* subjectivity
Shakespeare, William, 11
signification, 49, 63, 70, 96, 98-99, 112-13, 120, 125; and the other, 99; and the dialogical word, 100-09; and the face, 103-04; and expiation, 115; and spirit, 122, 123. *See also* meaning